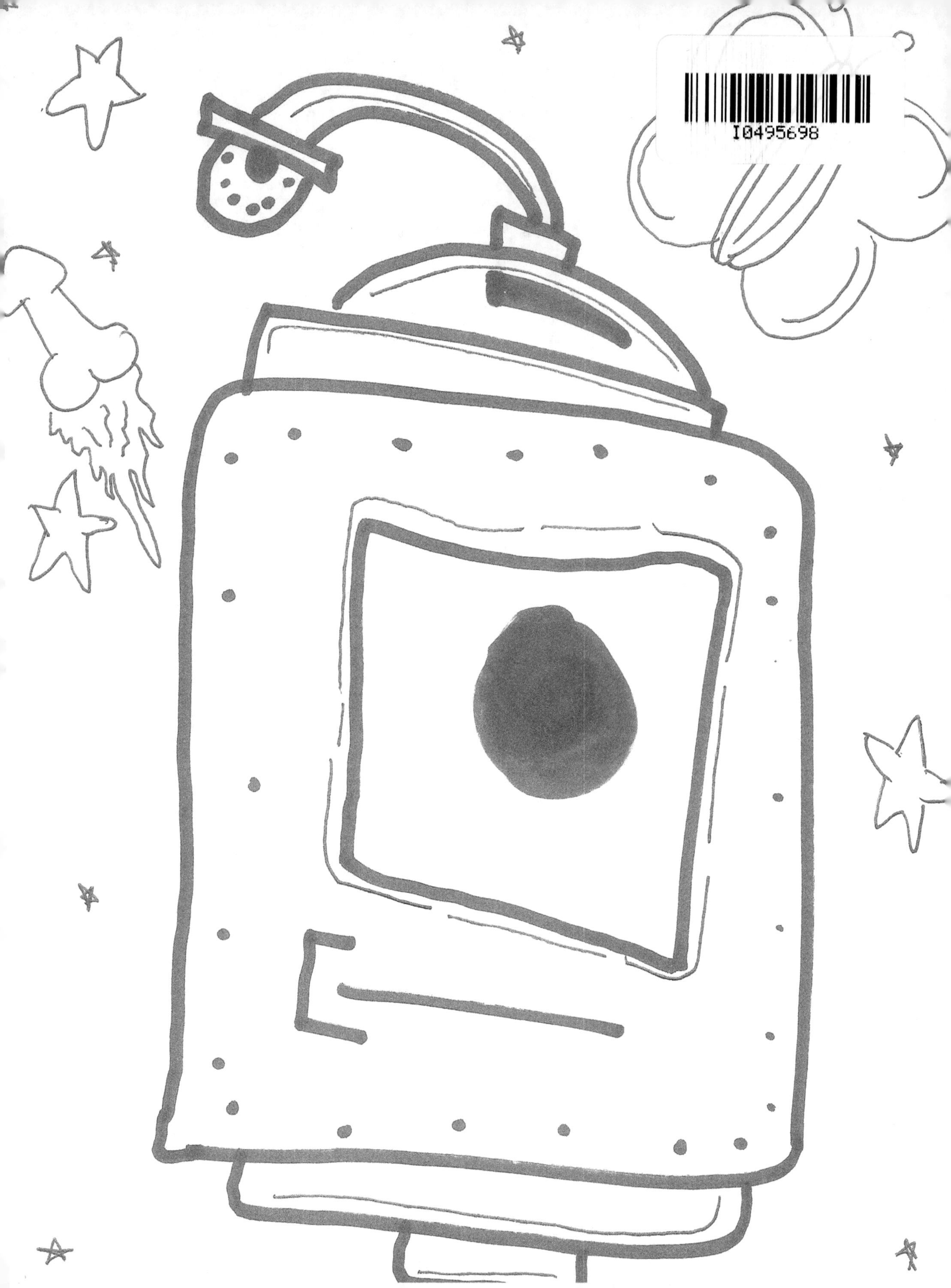

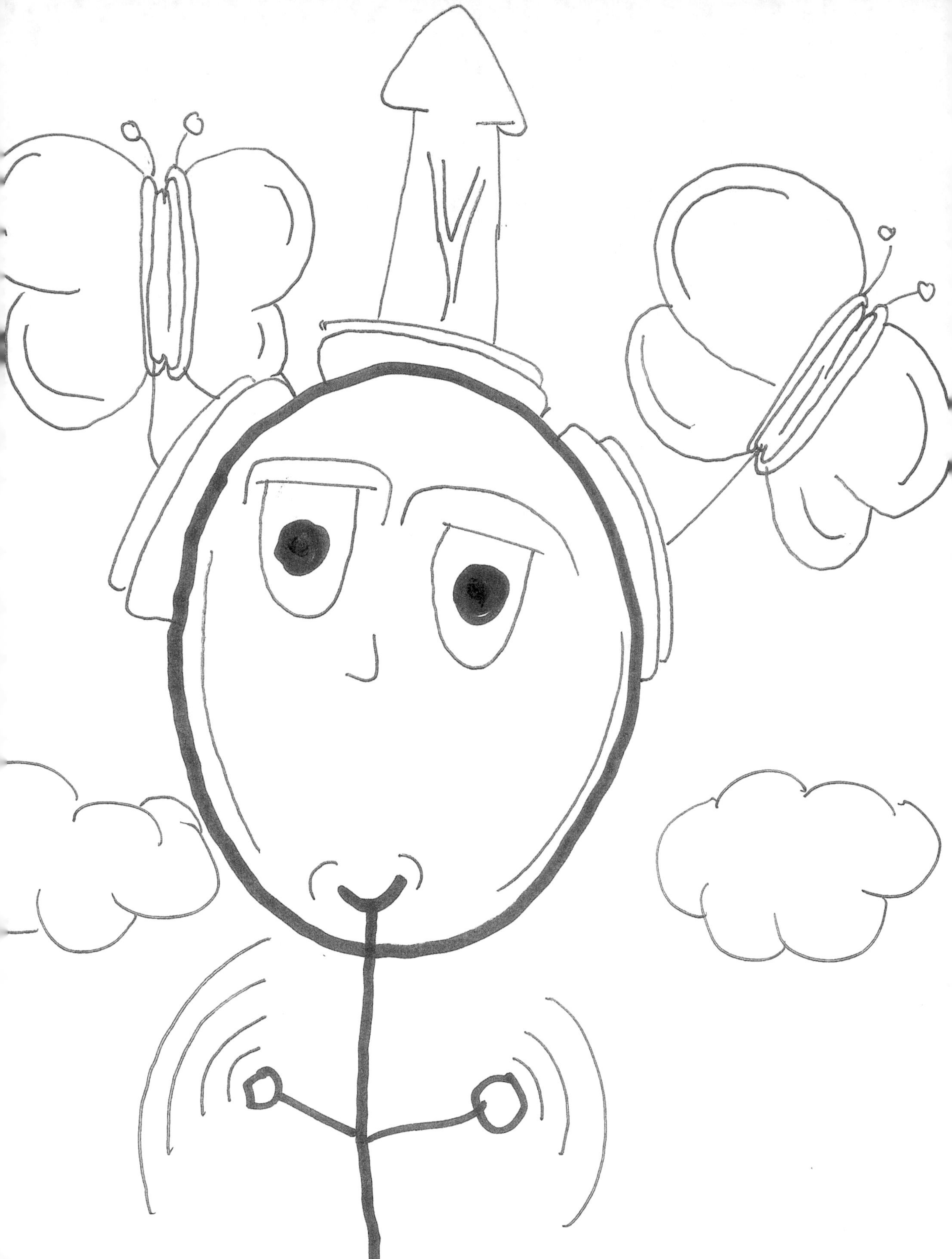

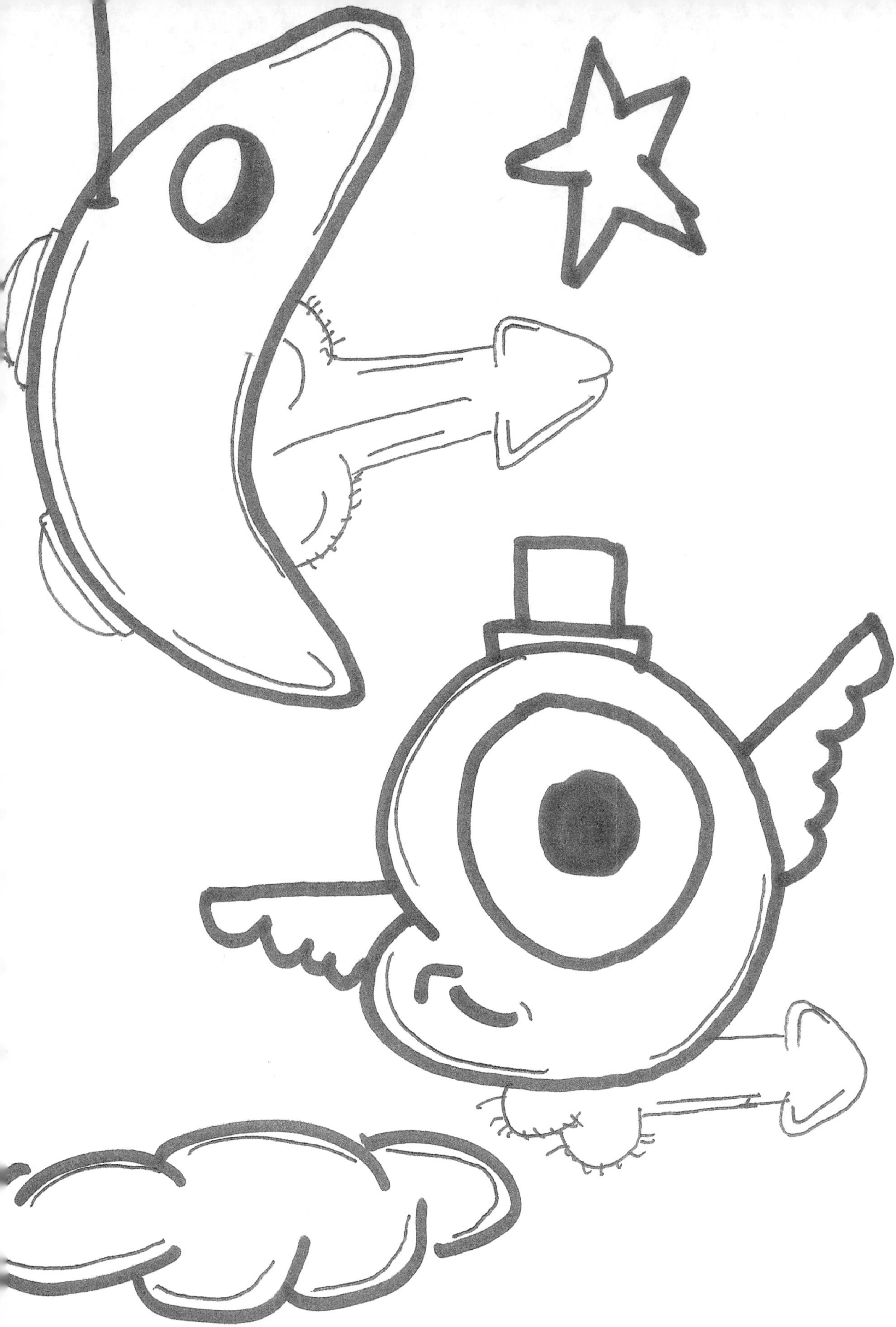

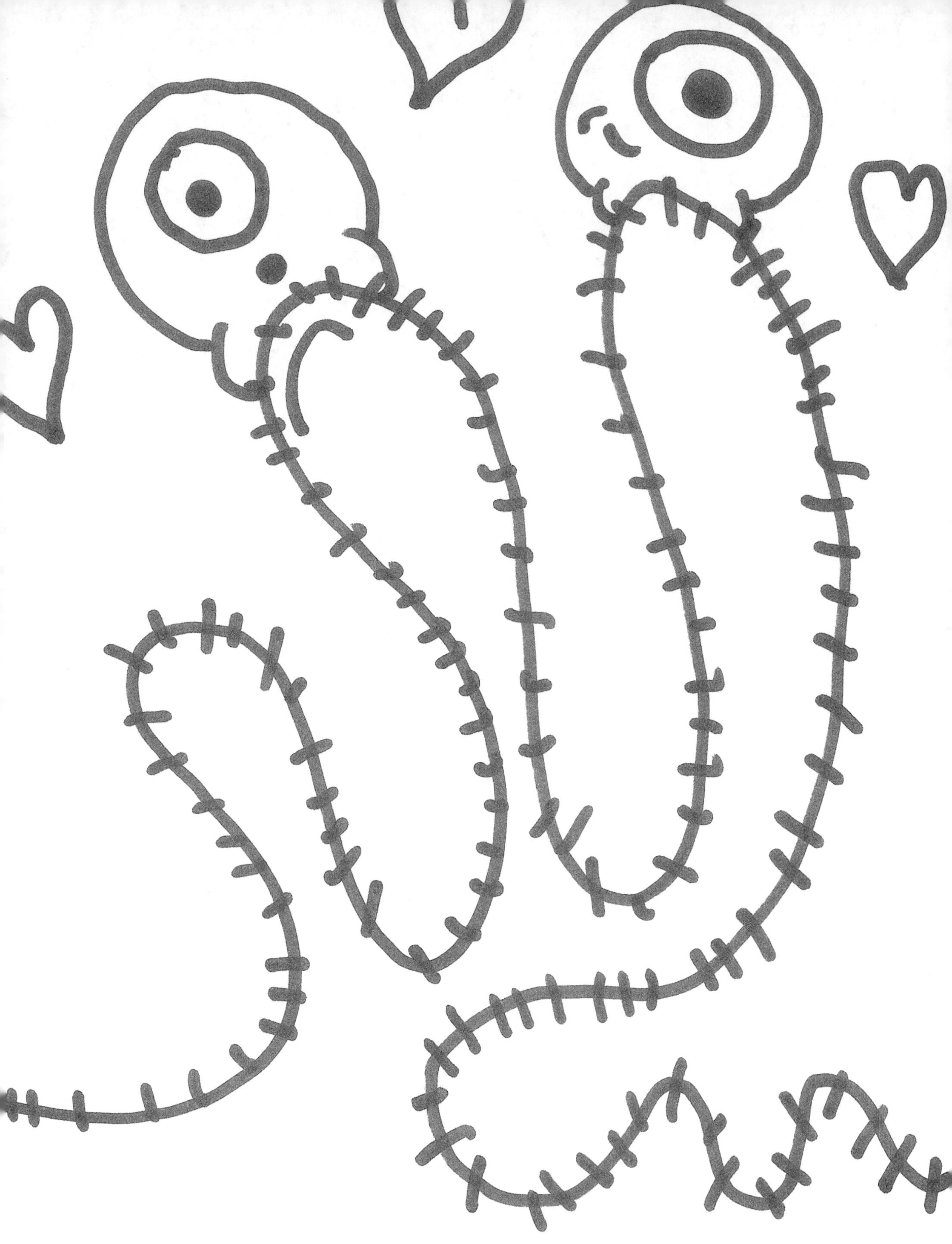

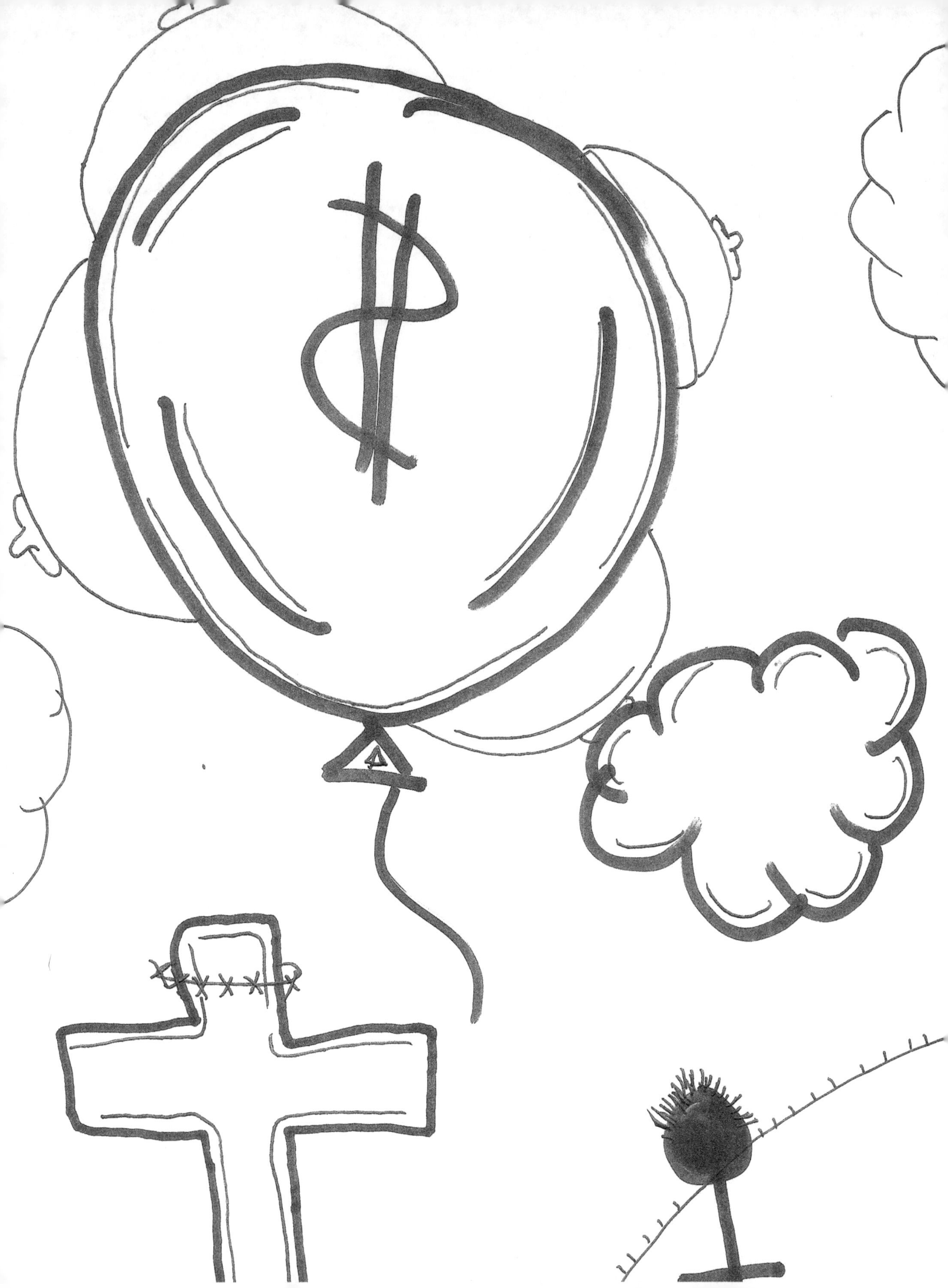

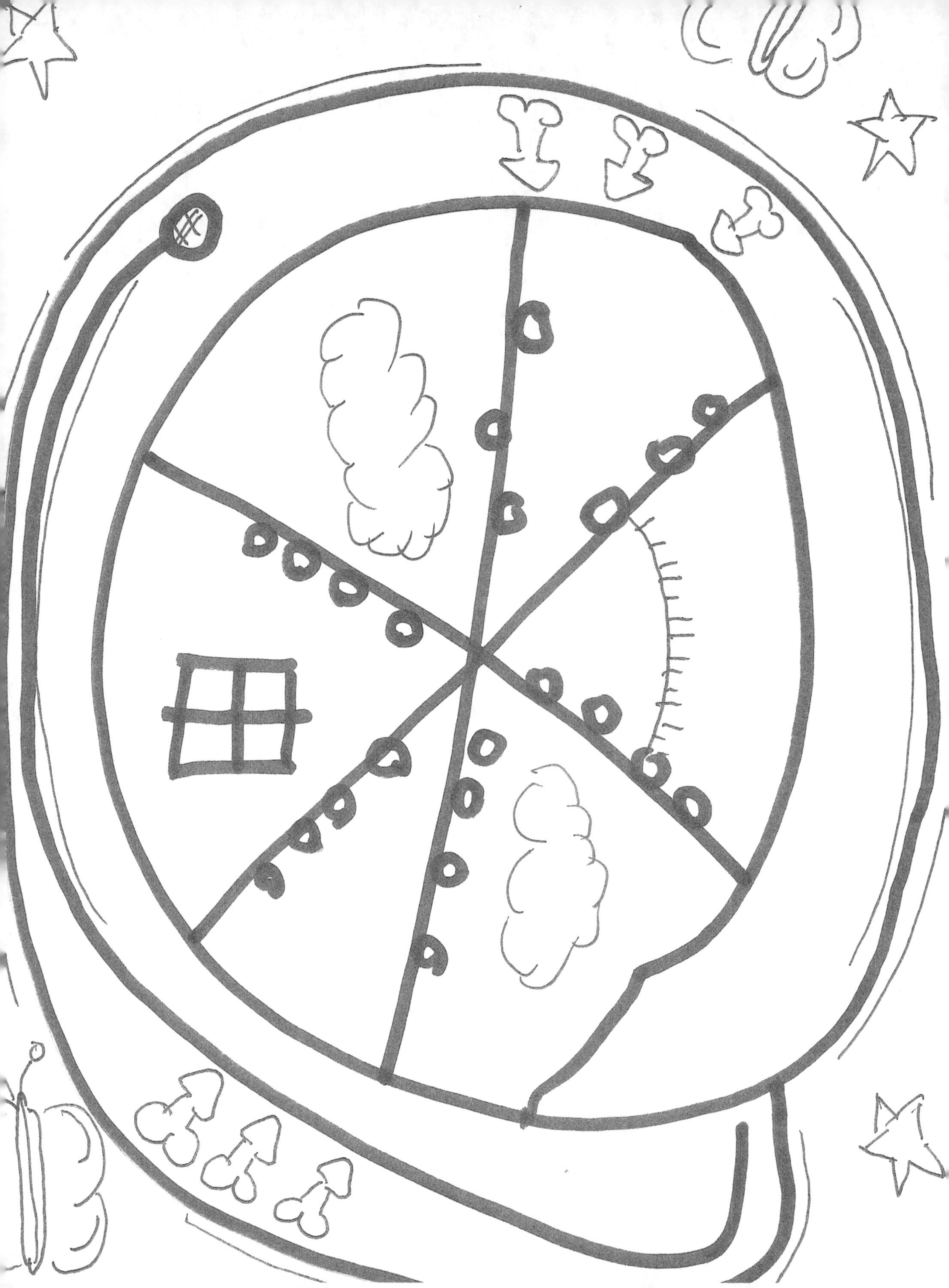

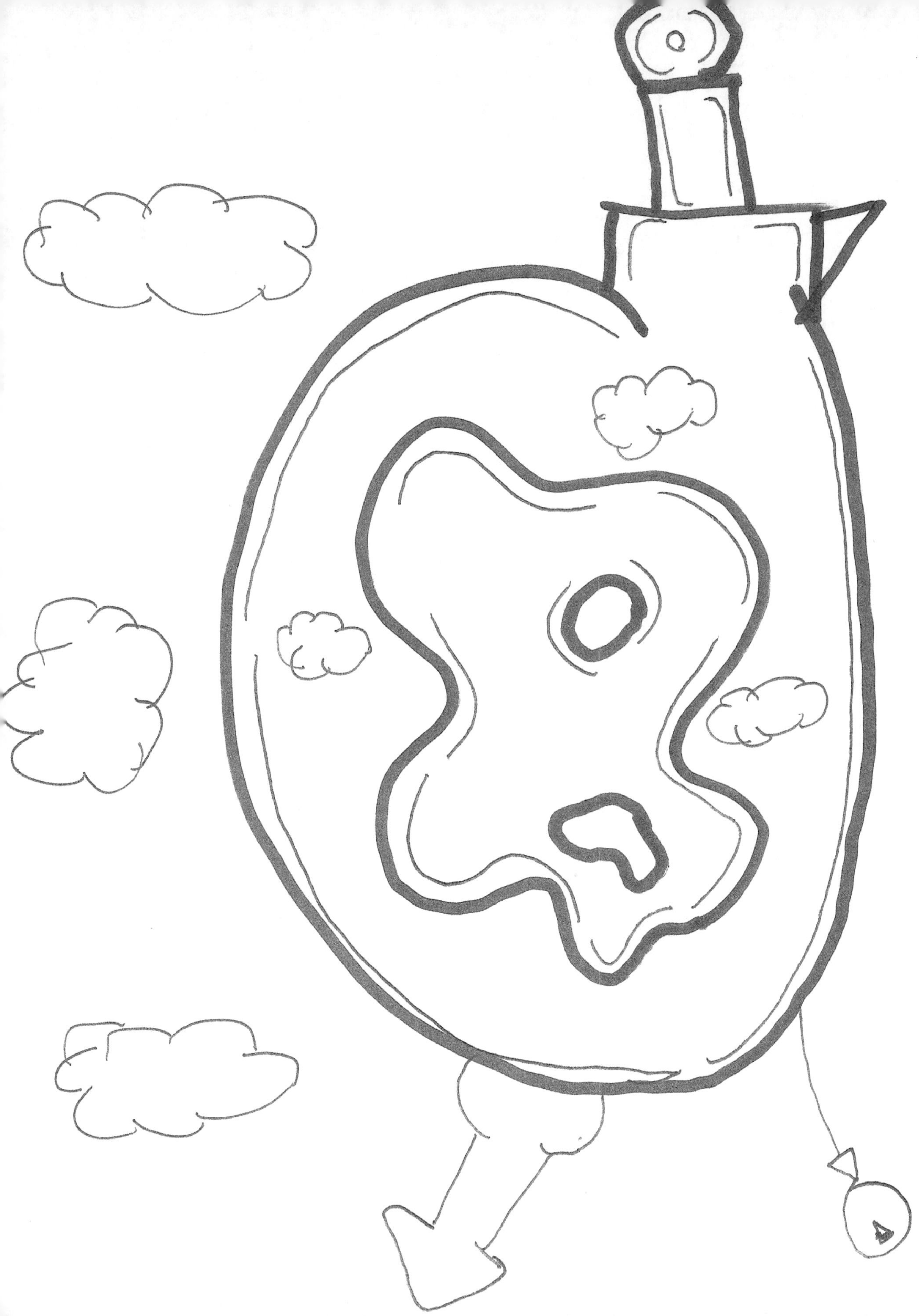

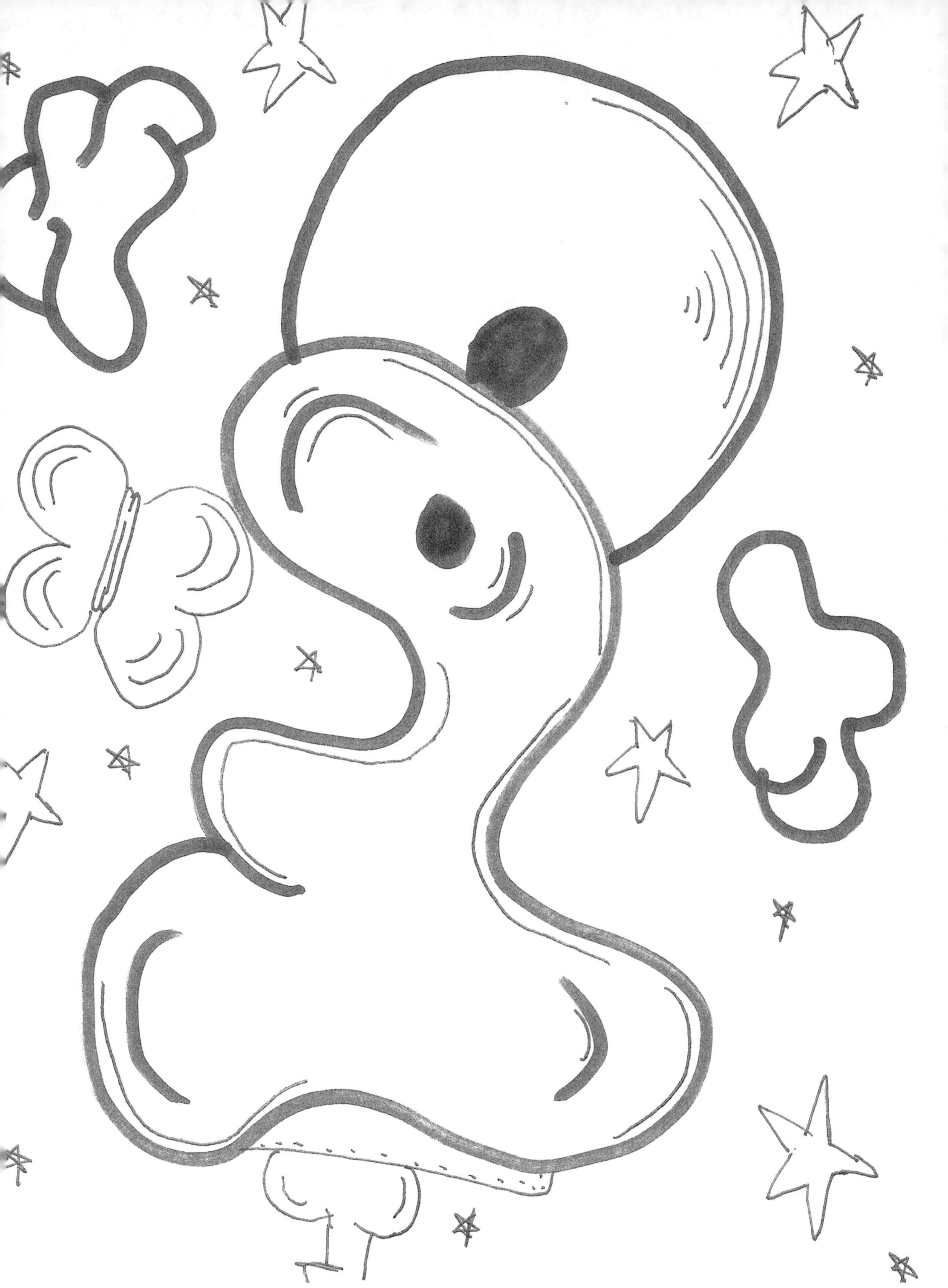

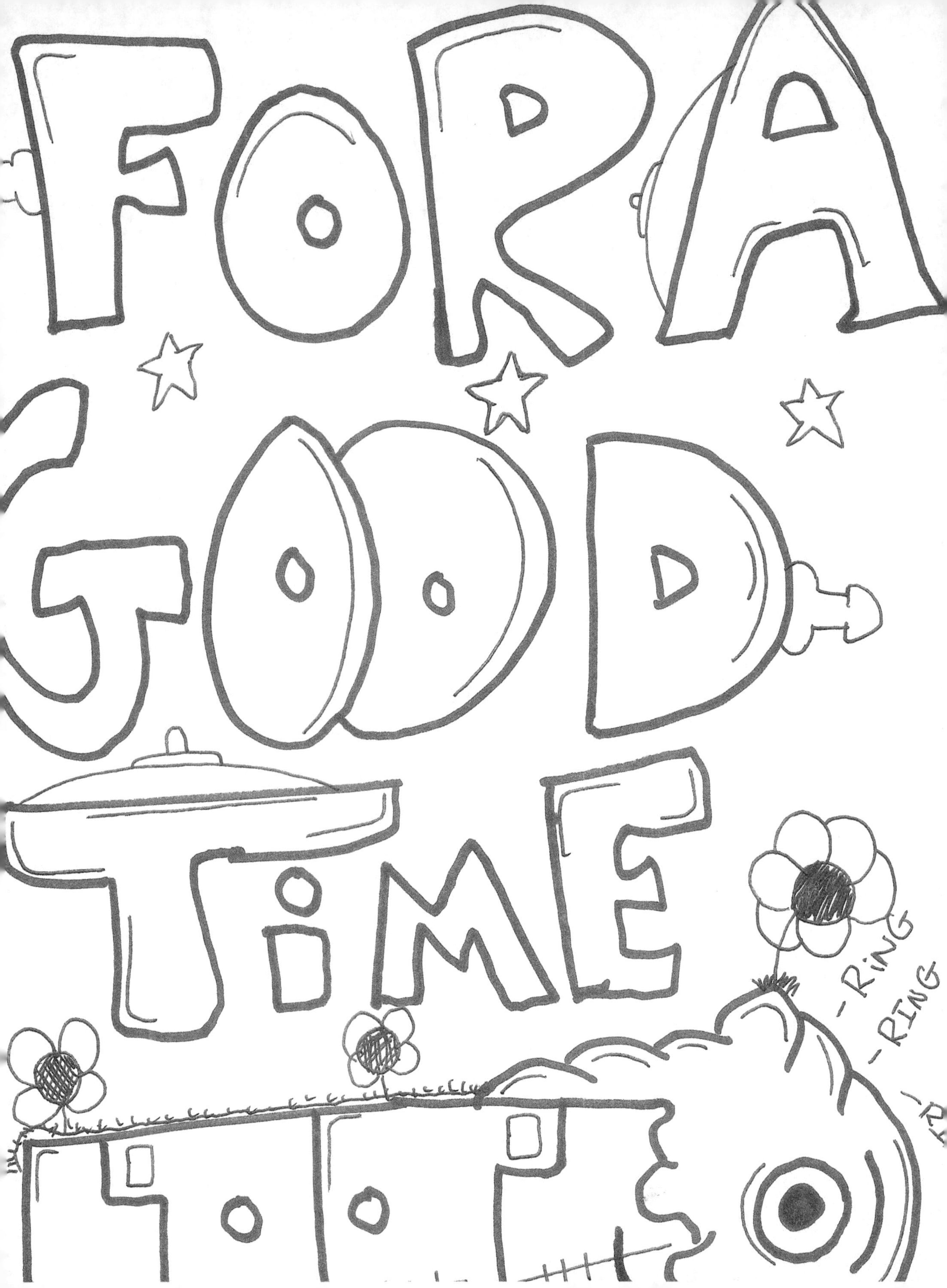
FOR A
GOOD
TIME
-RING
-RING

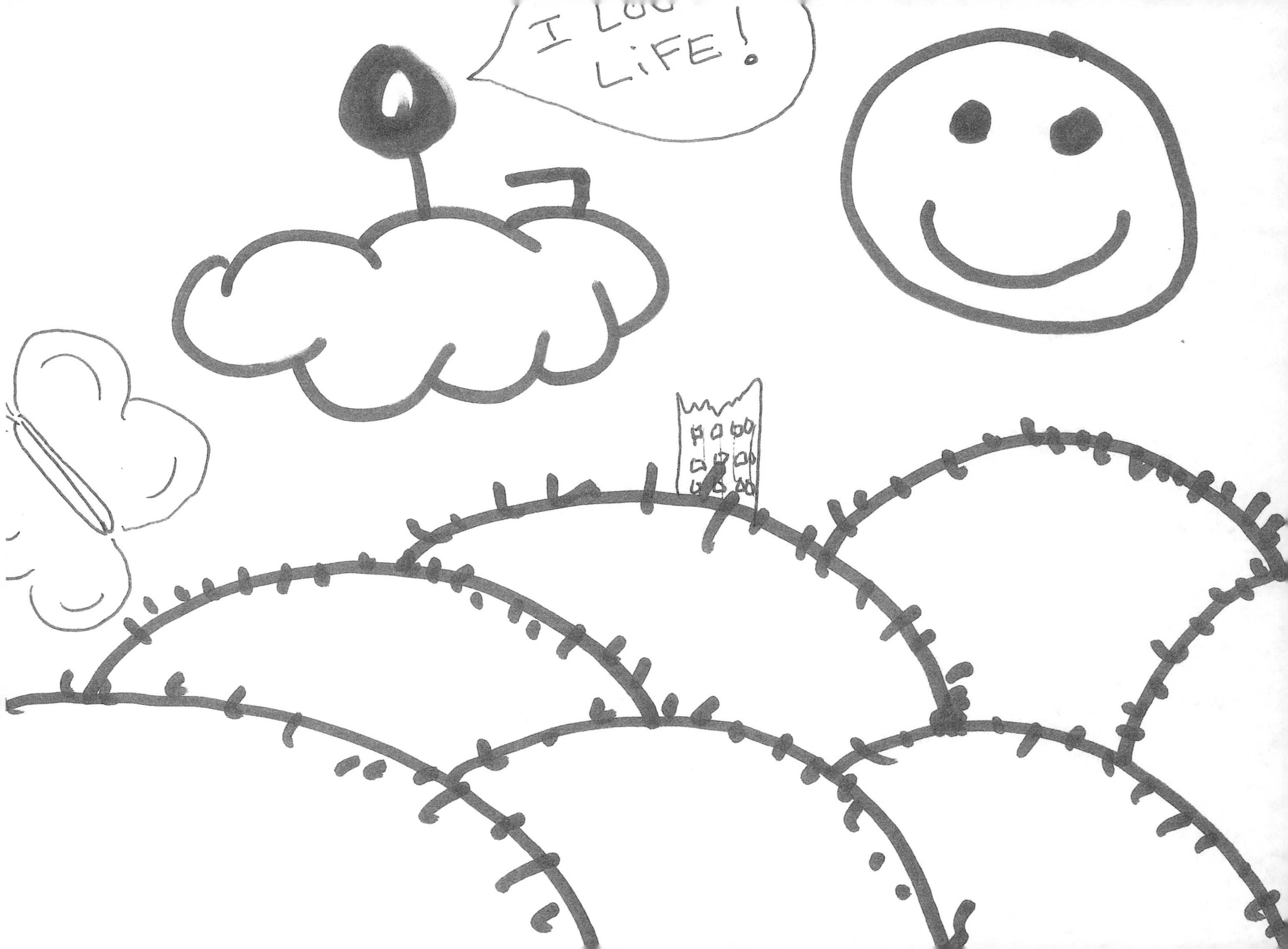
I LO
LiFE!

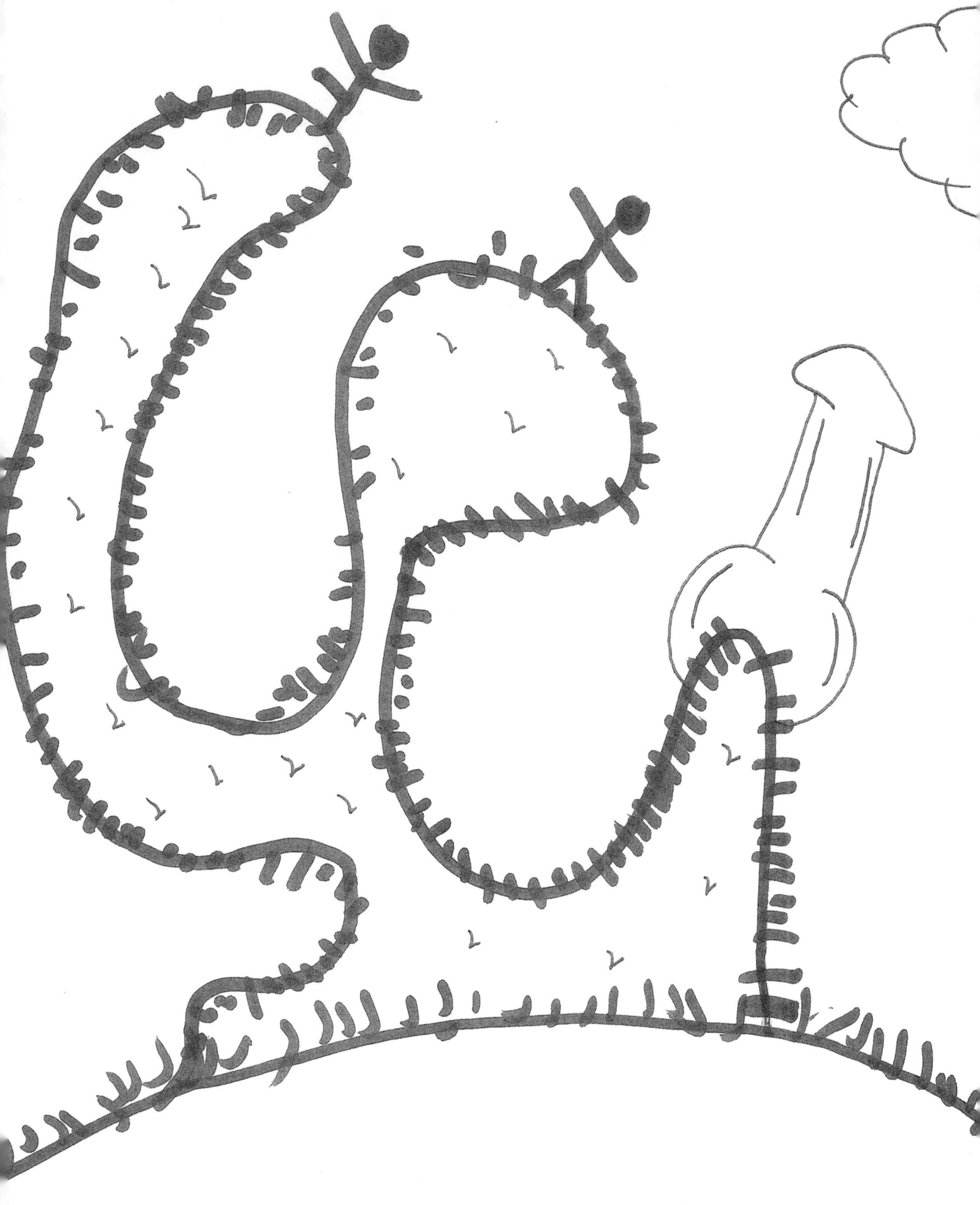

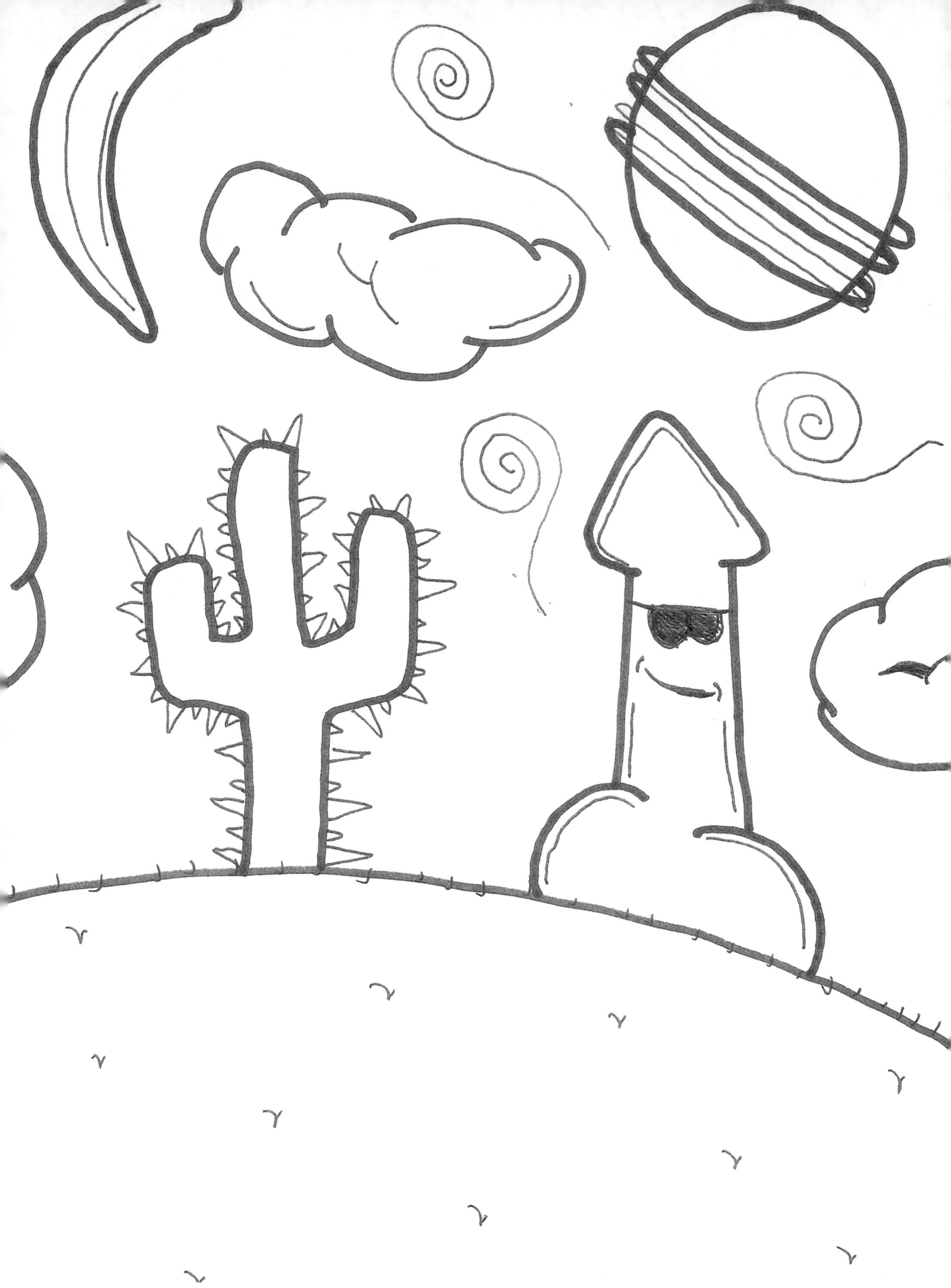

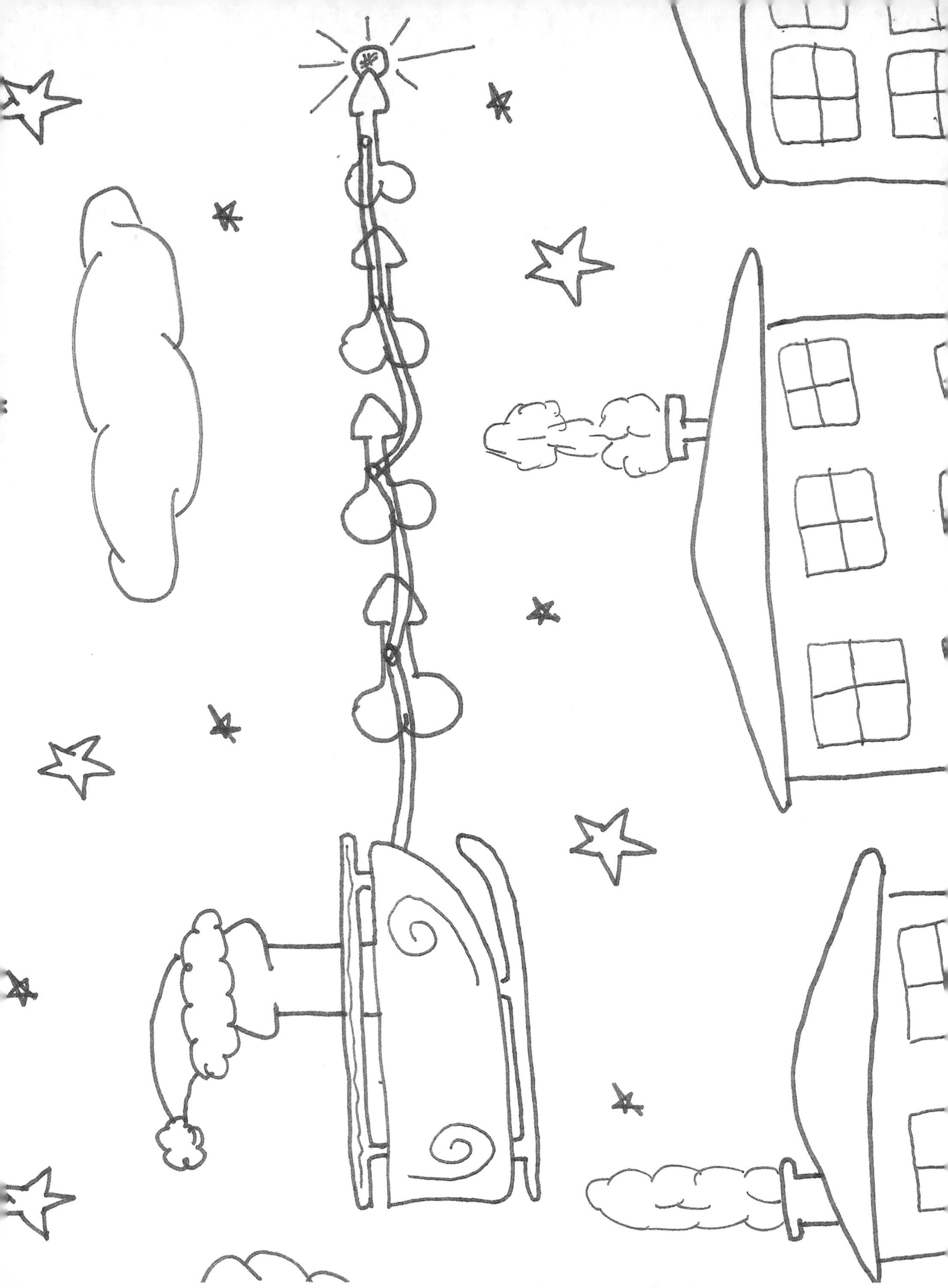

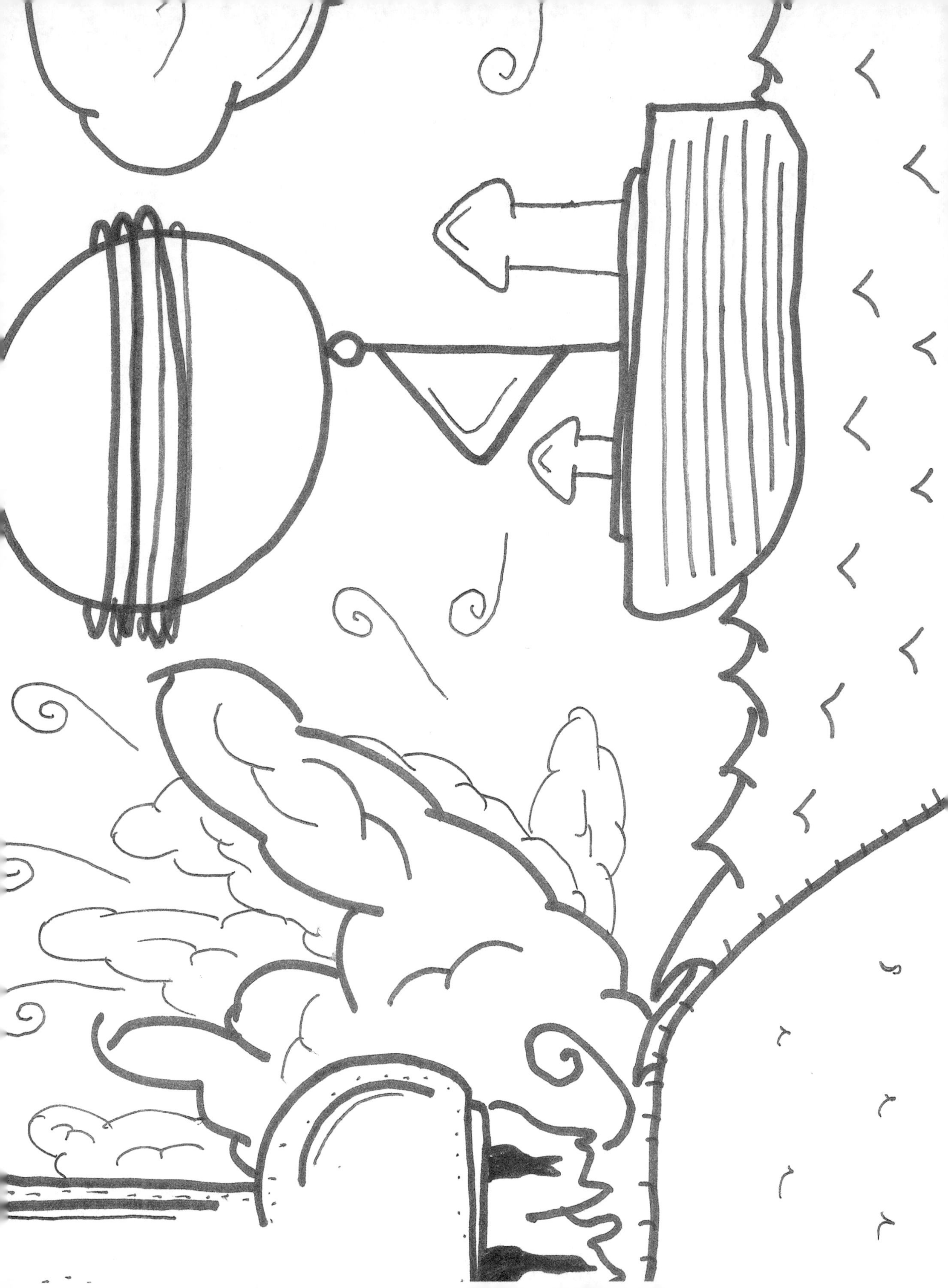

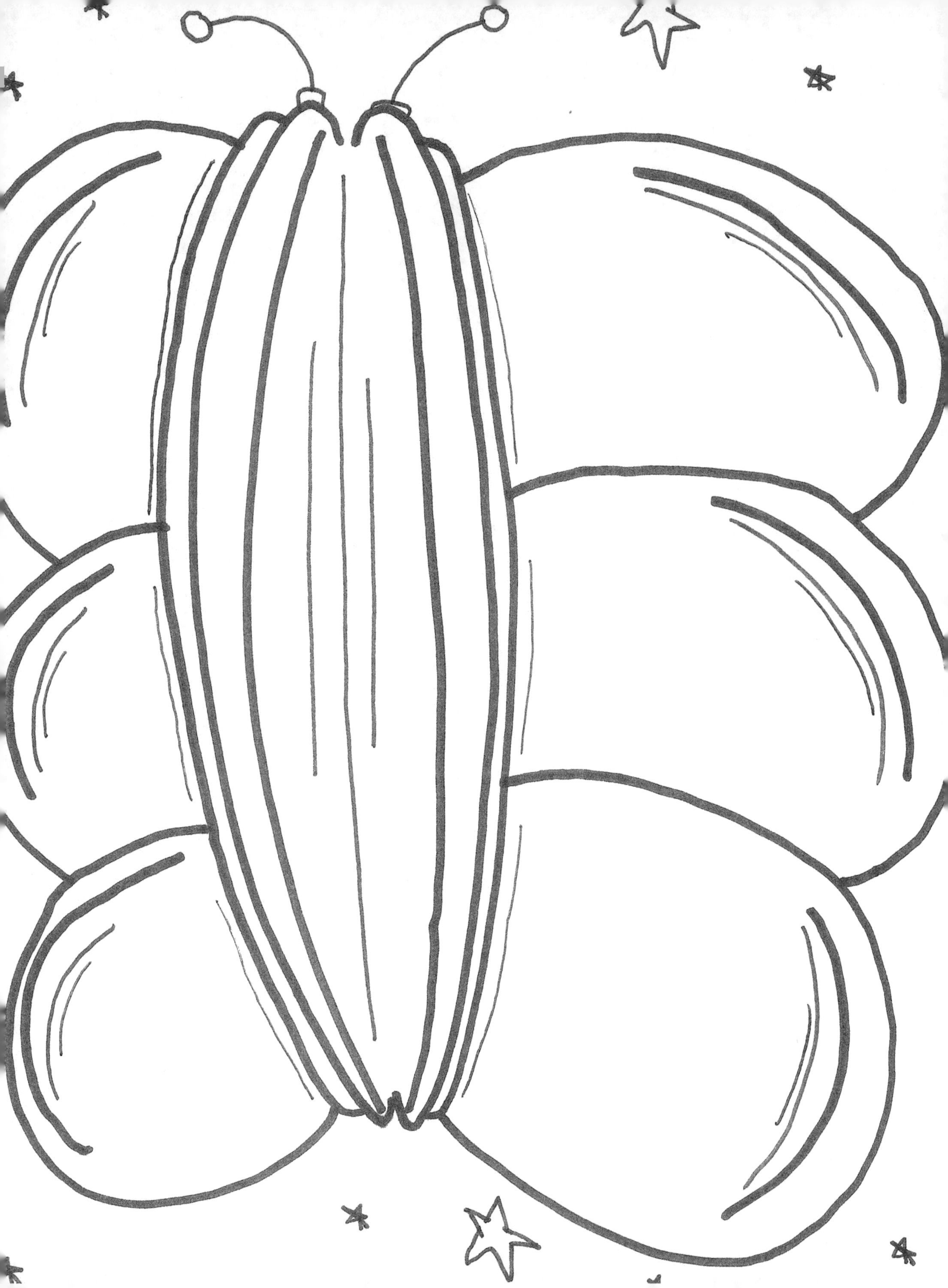

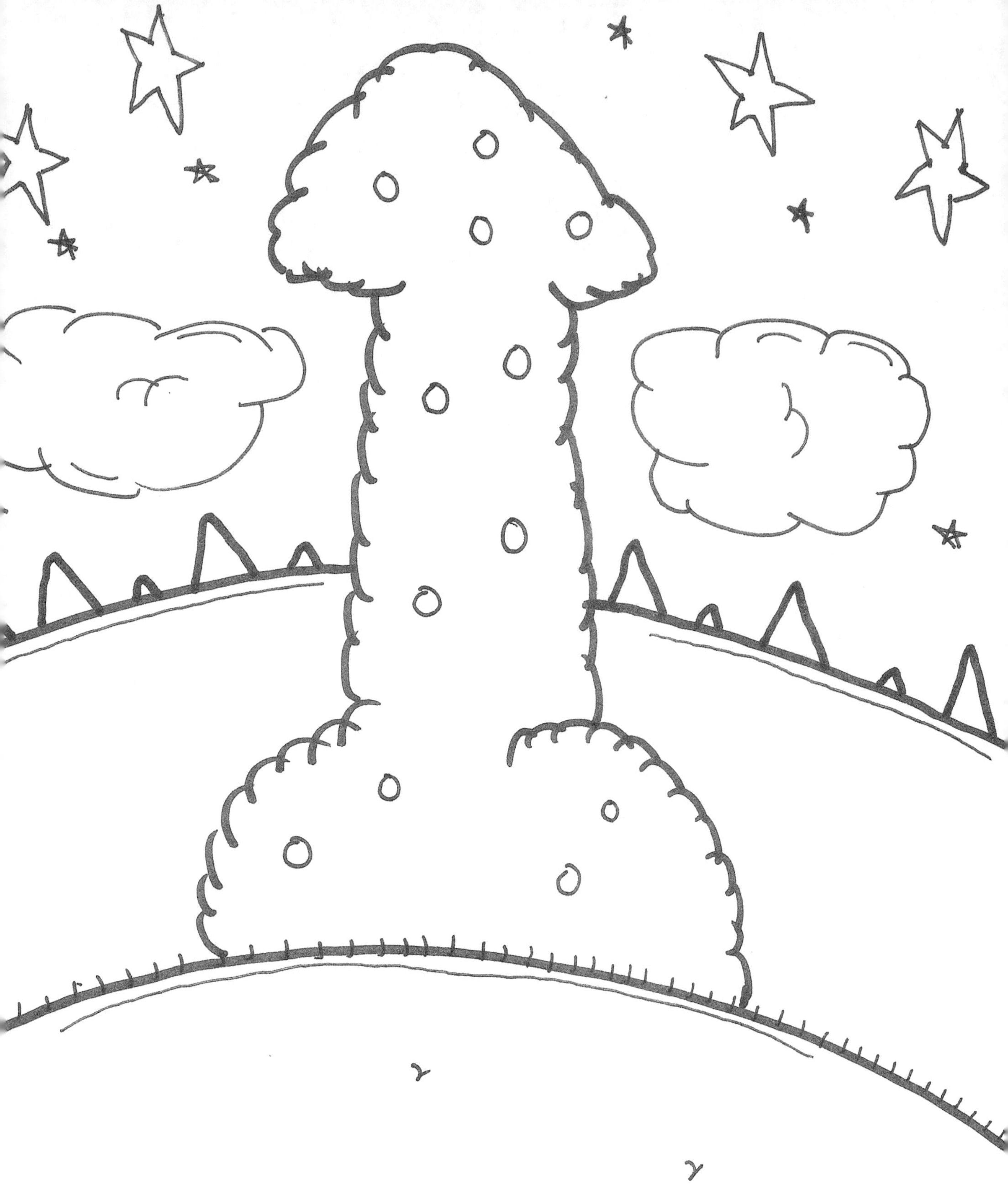

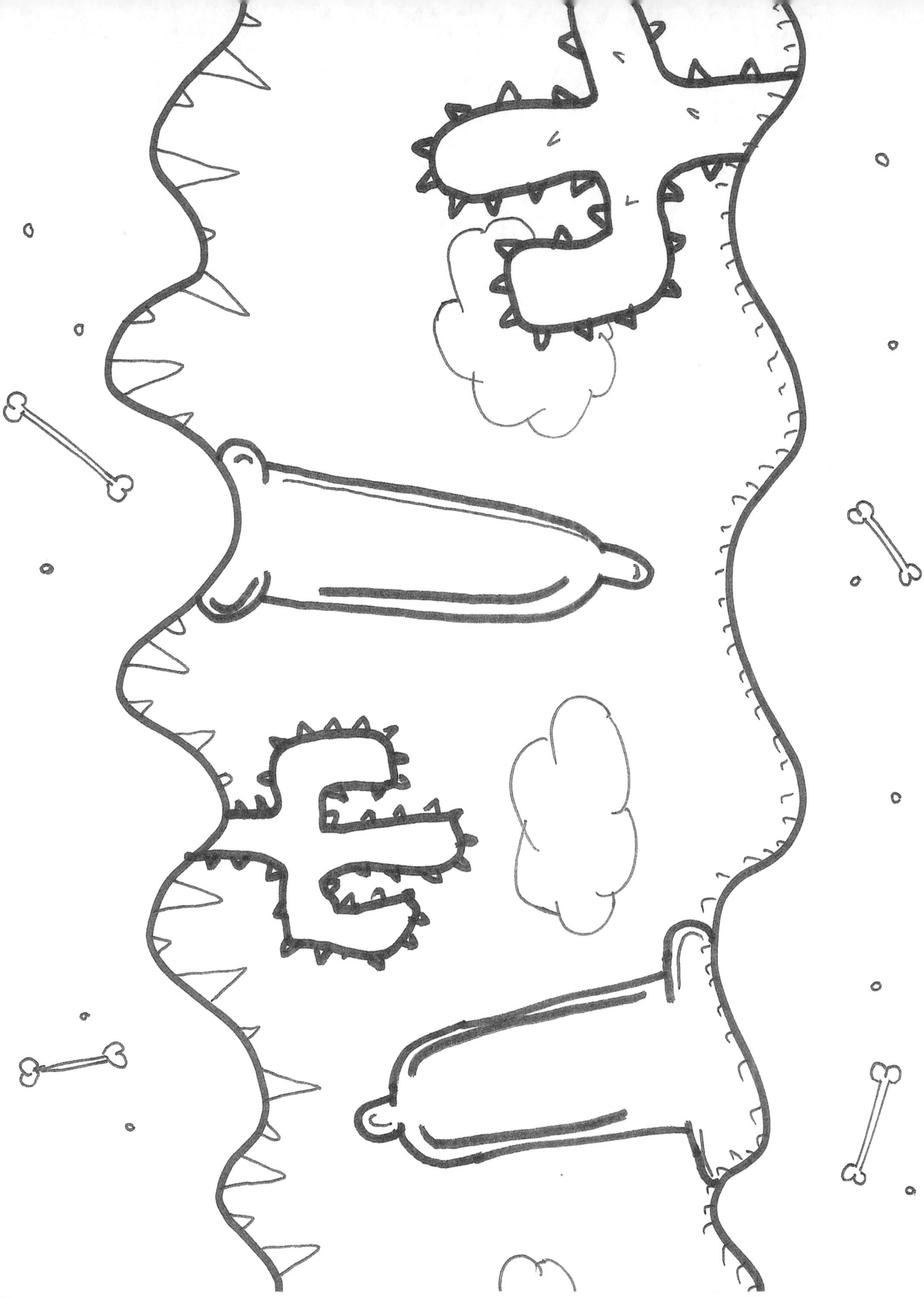

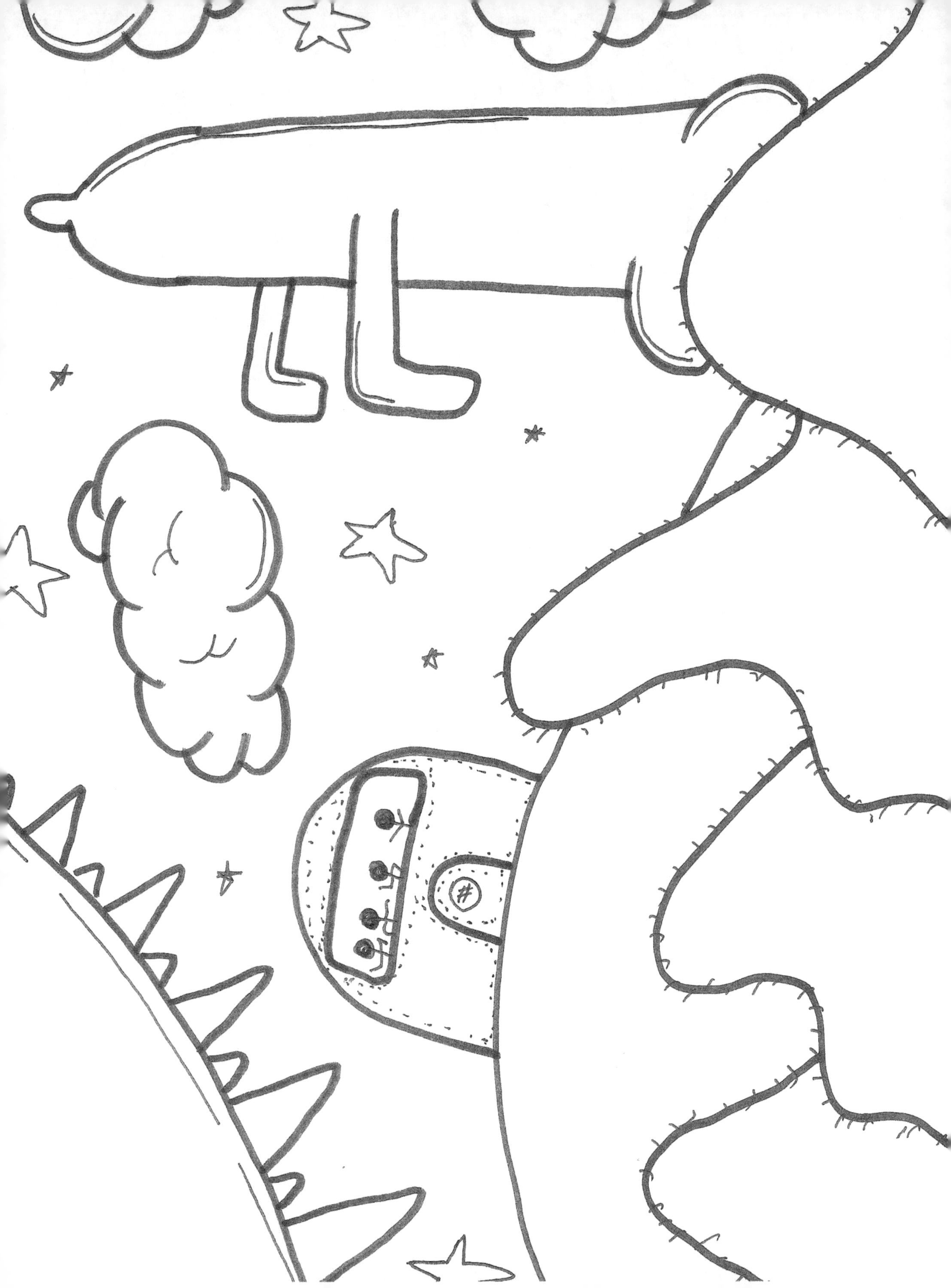

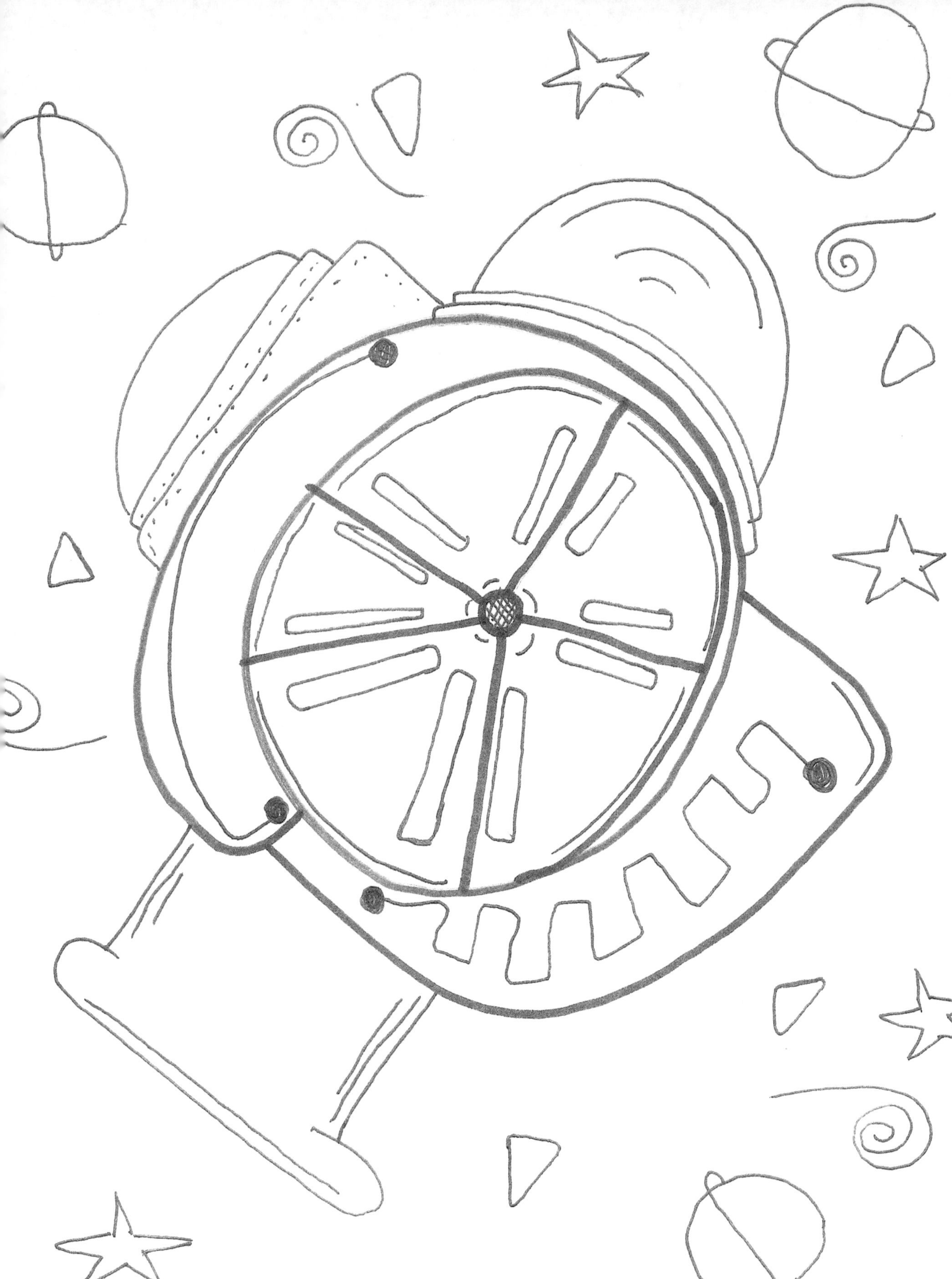

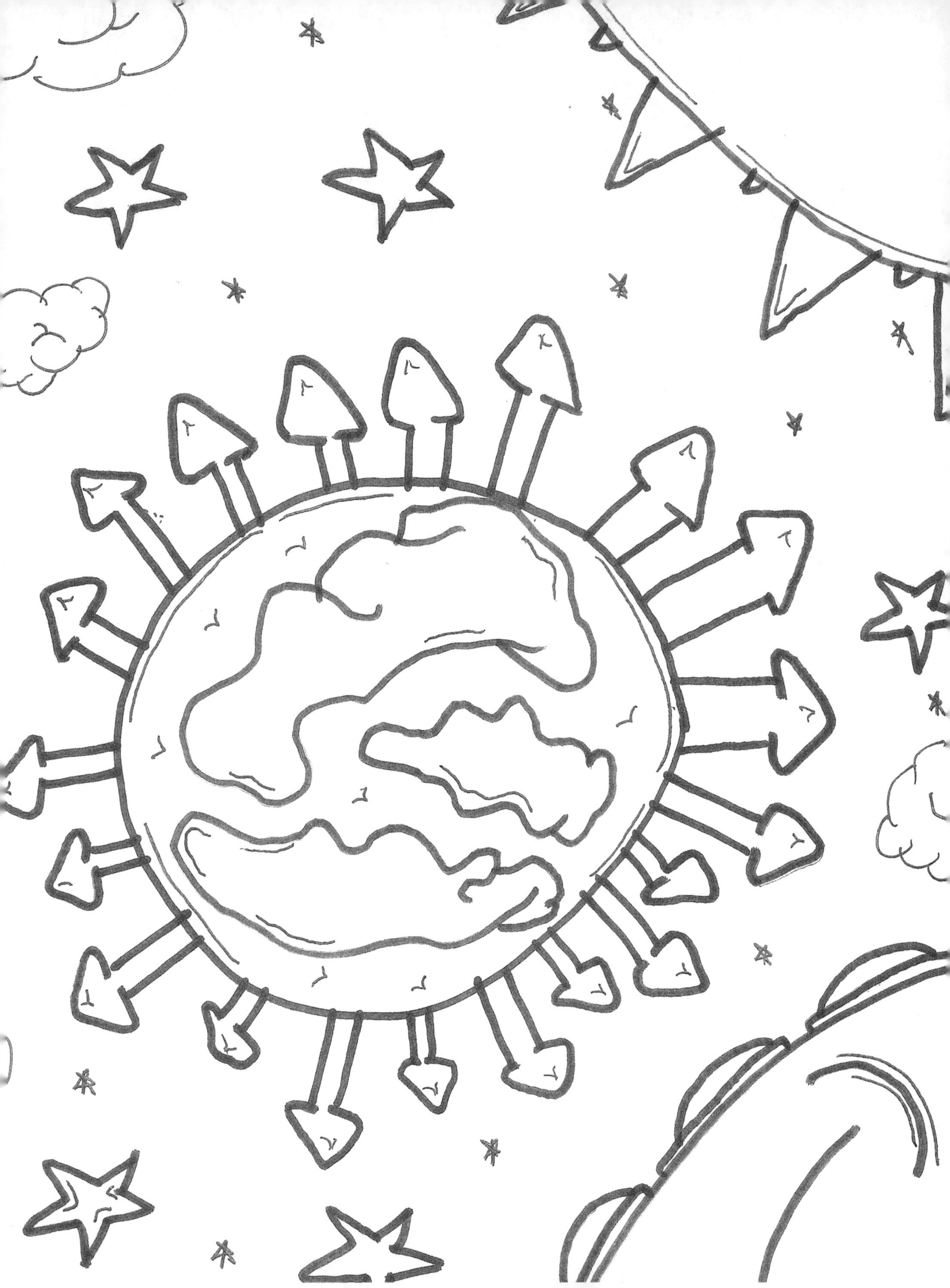

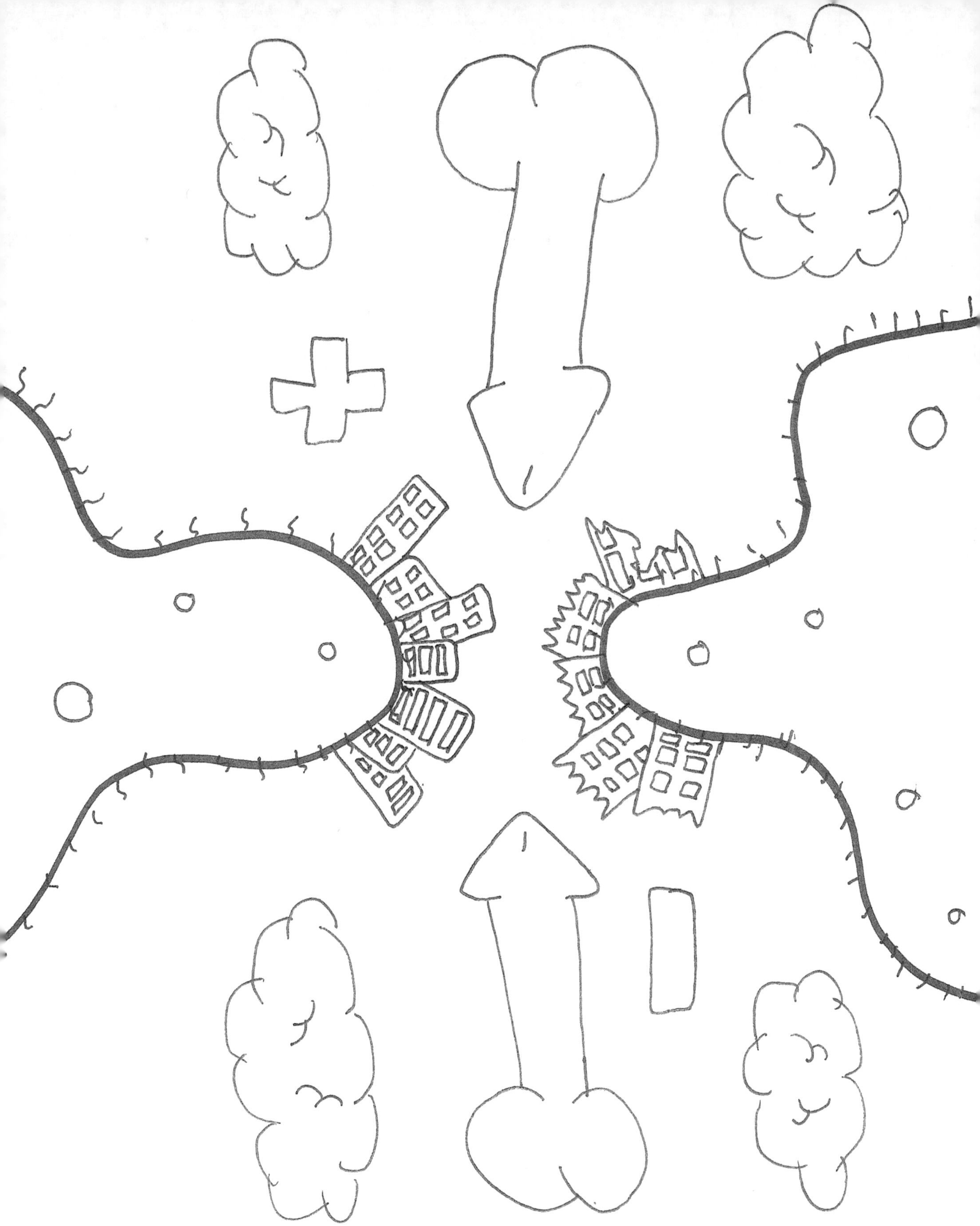

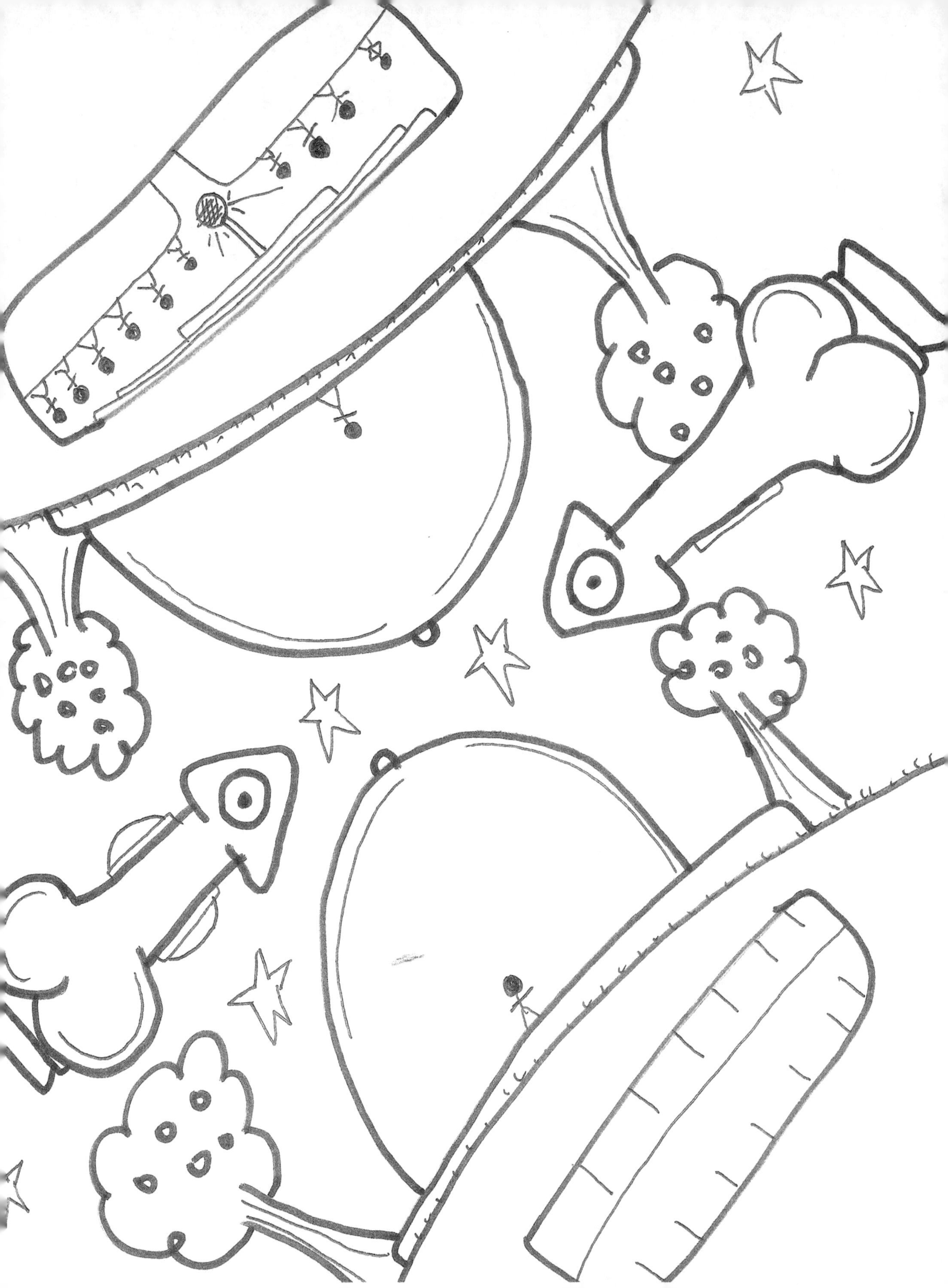

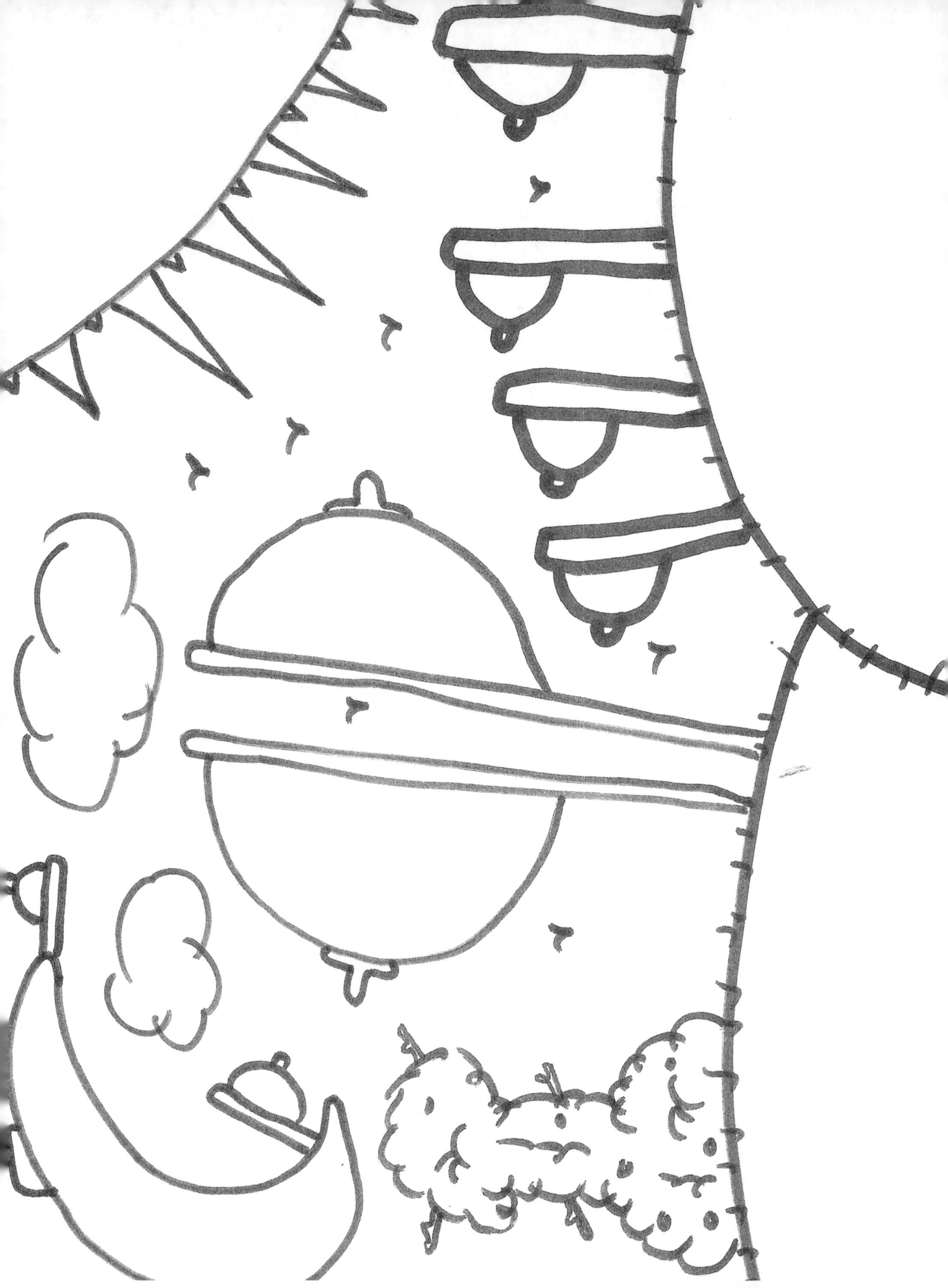

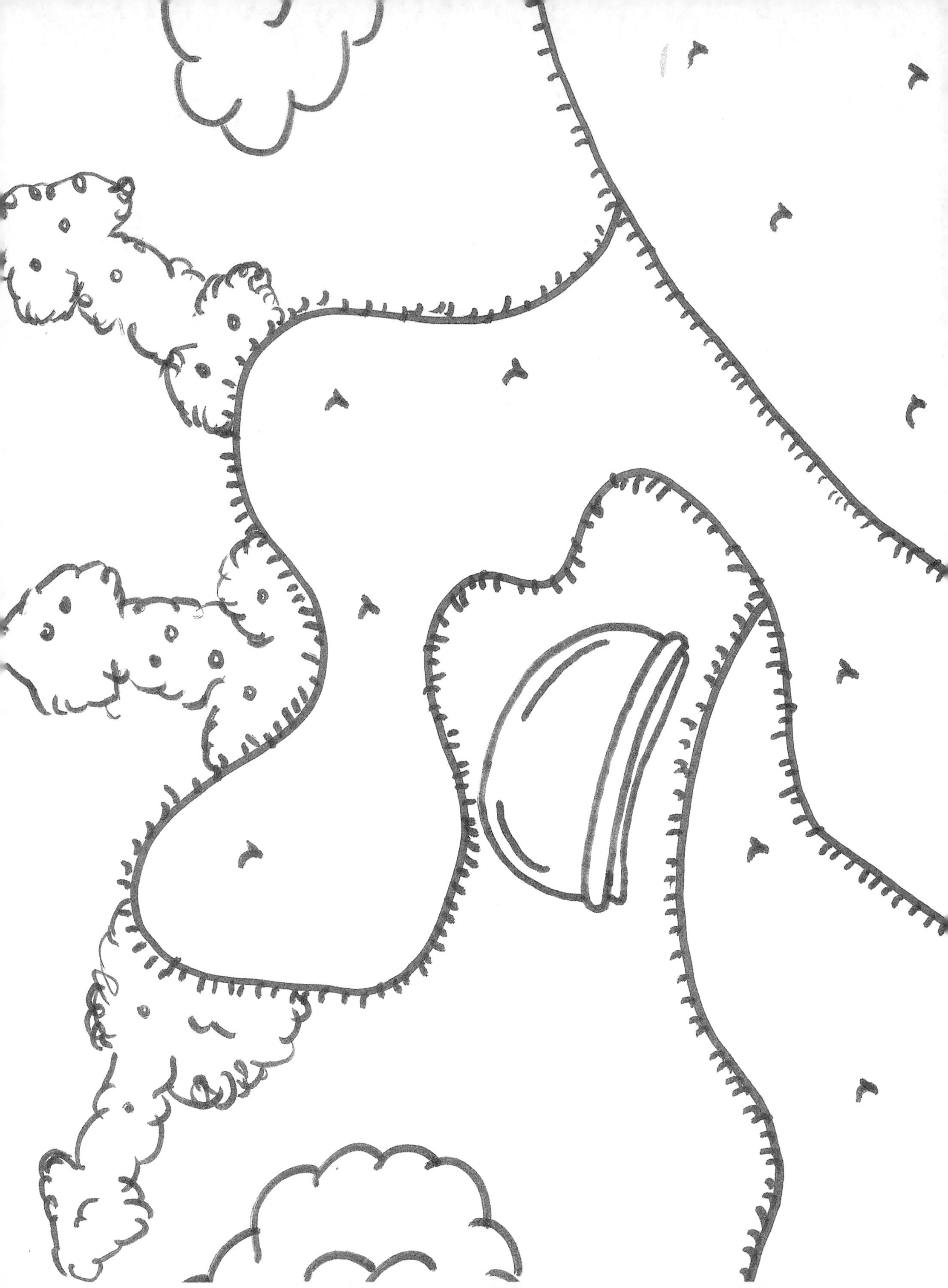

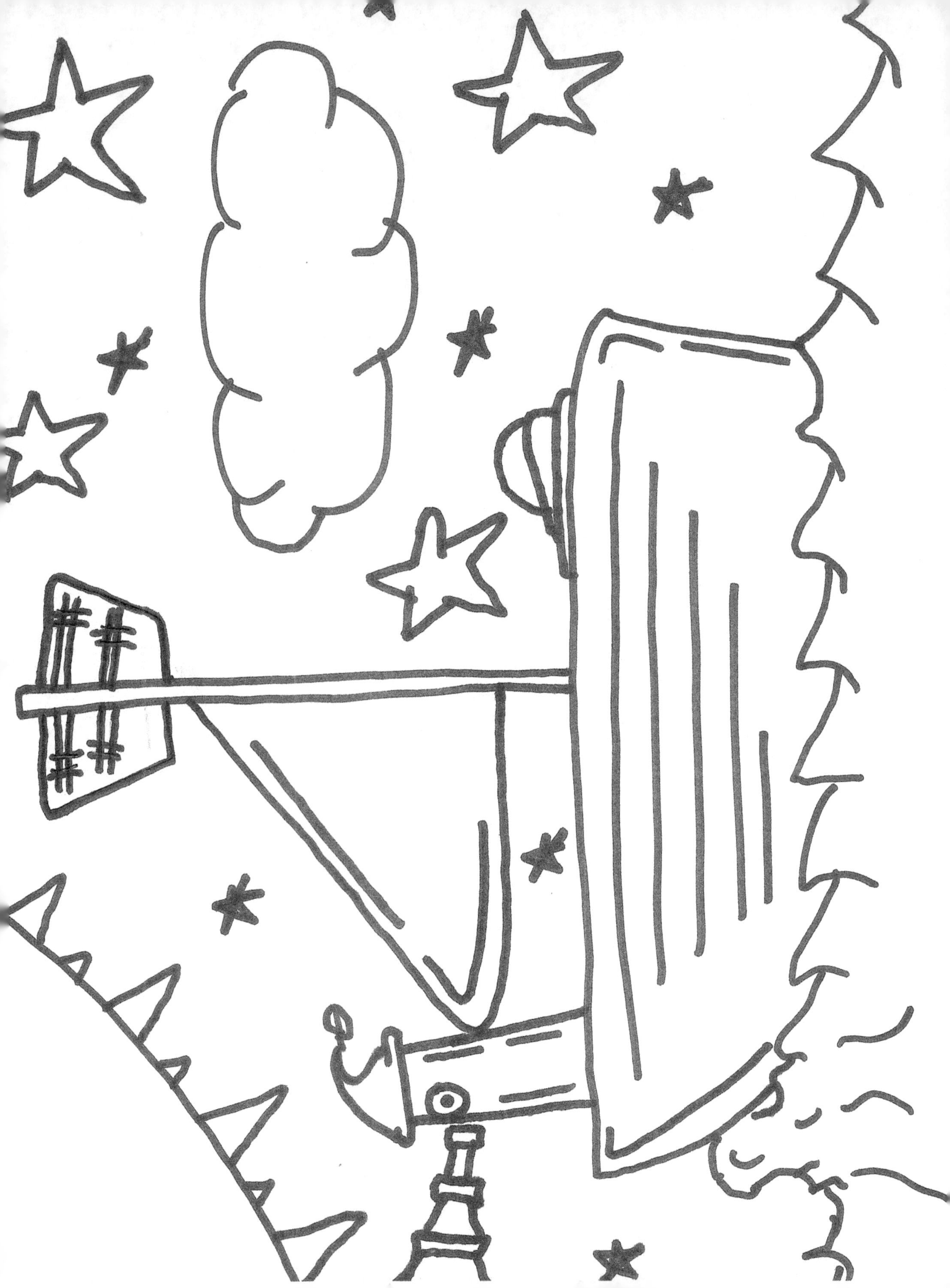

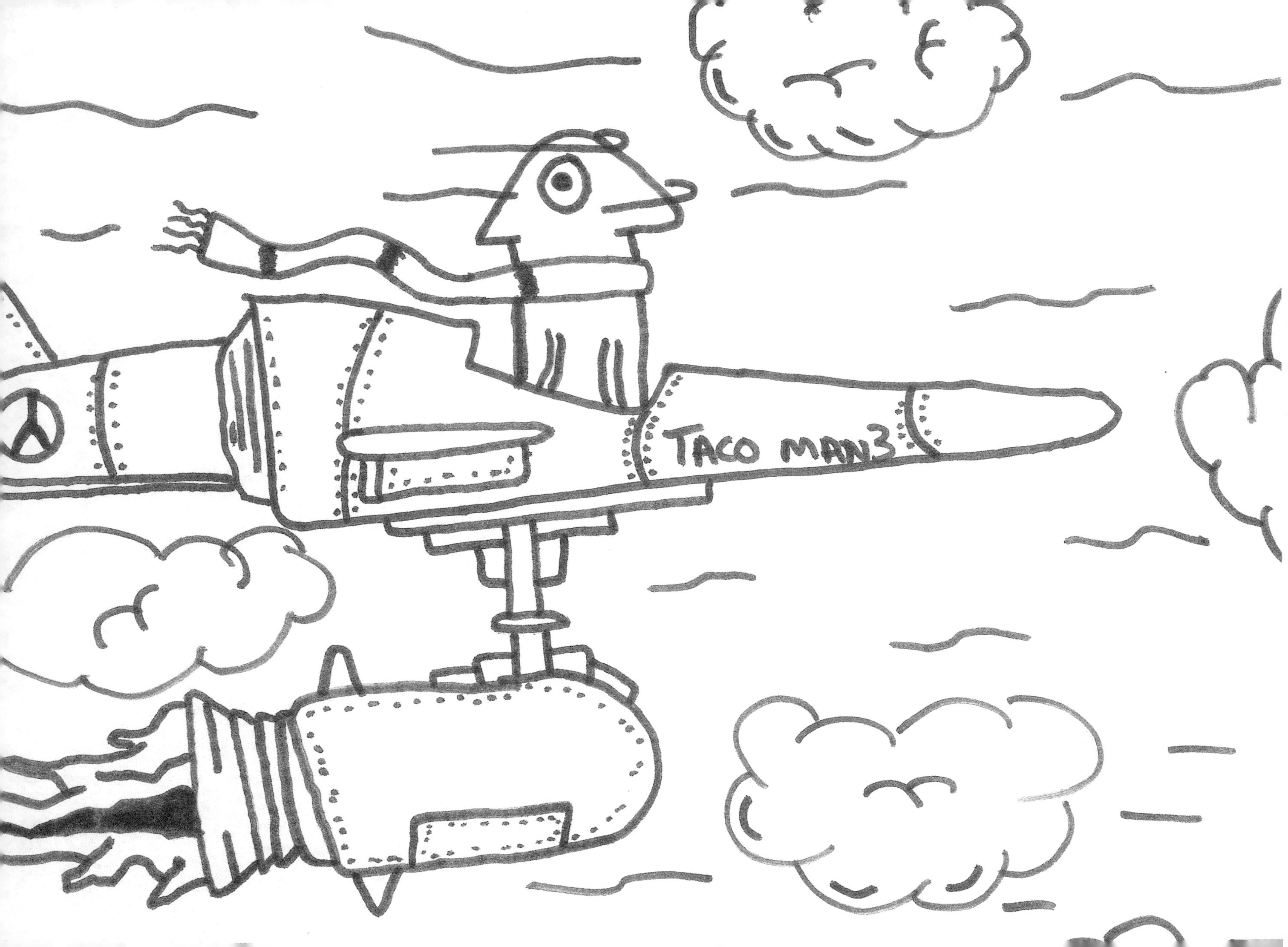
TACO MAN3

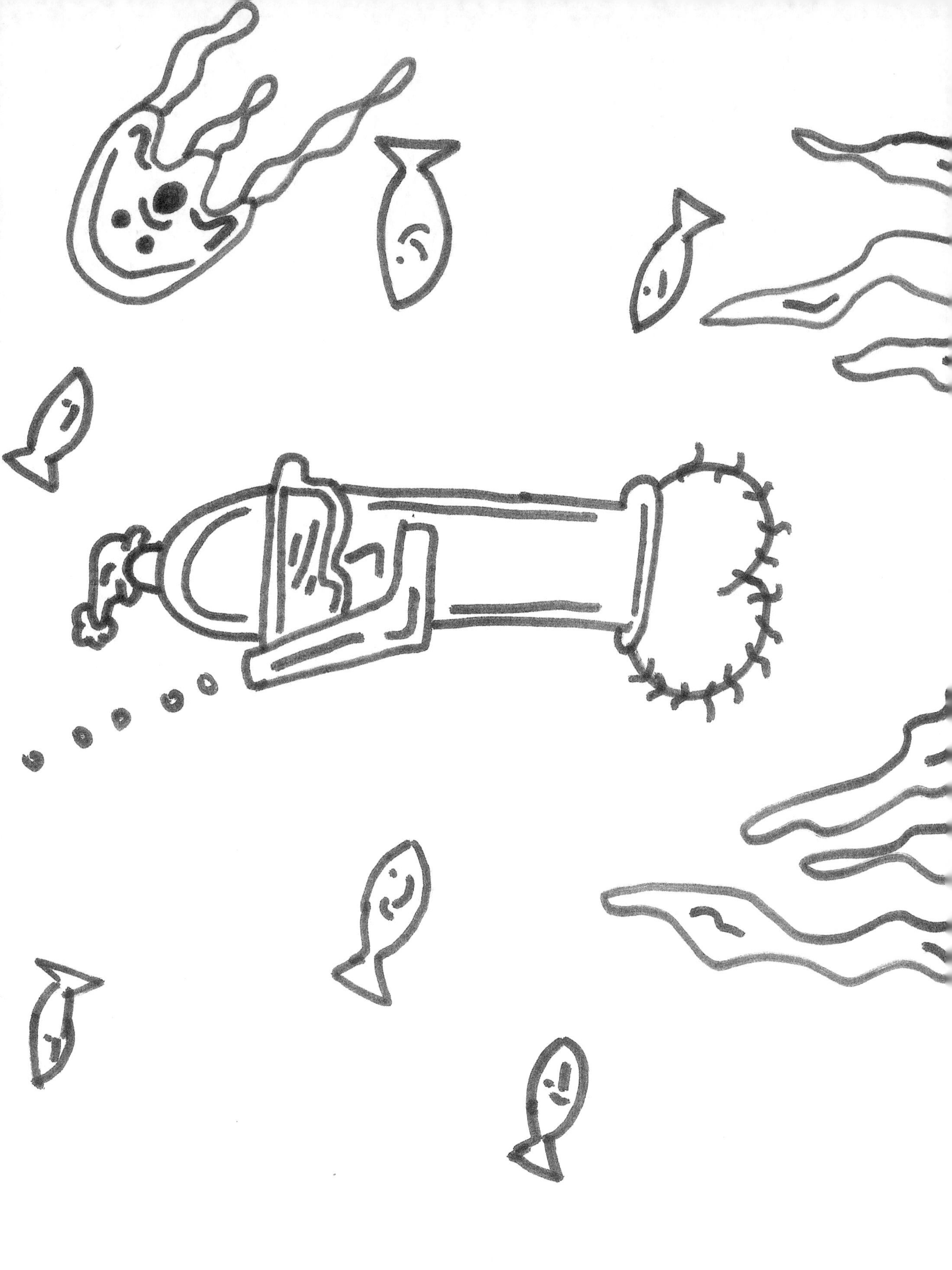

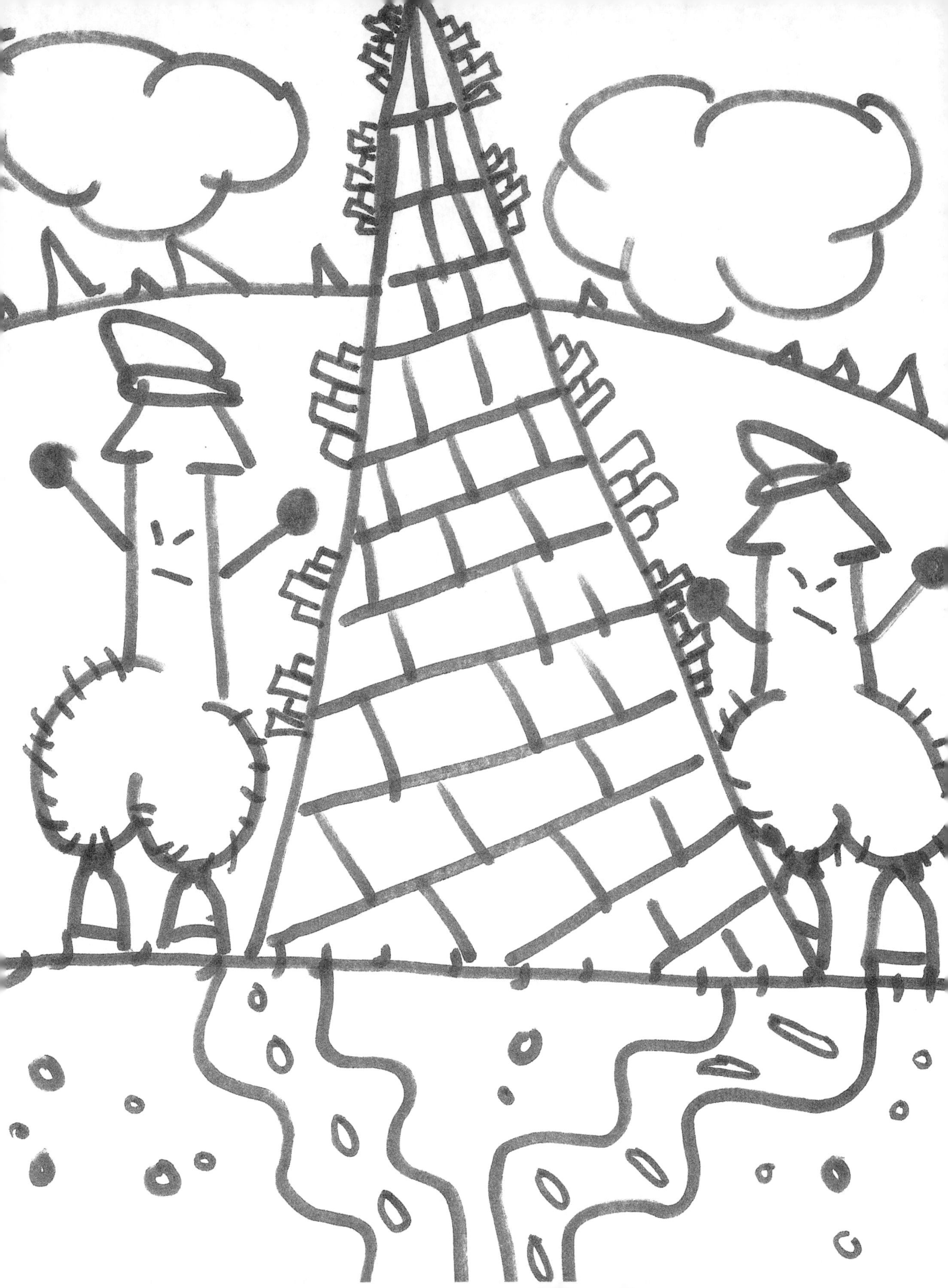

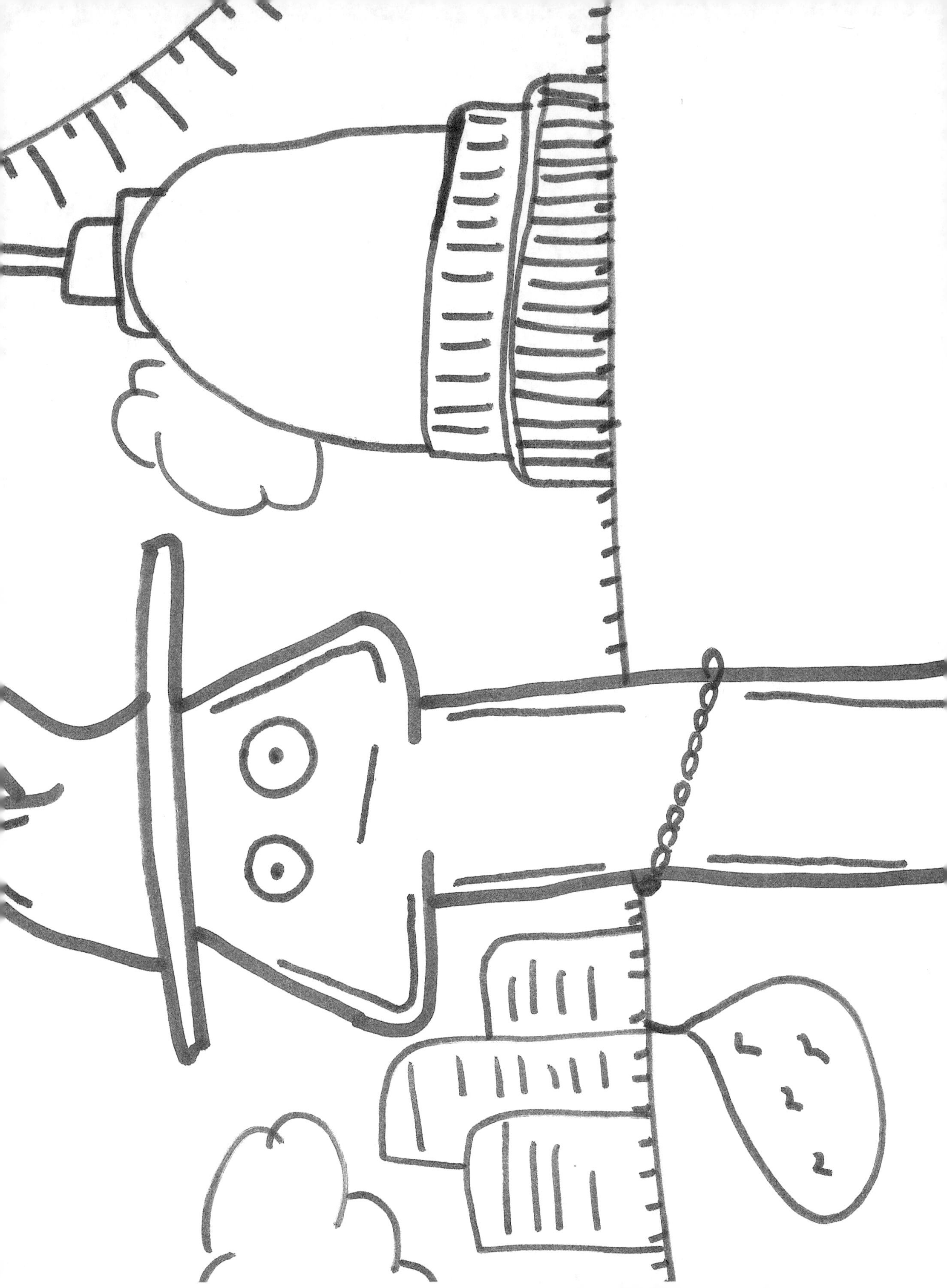

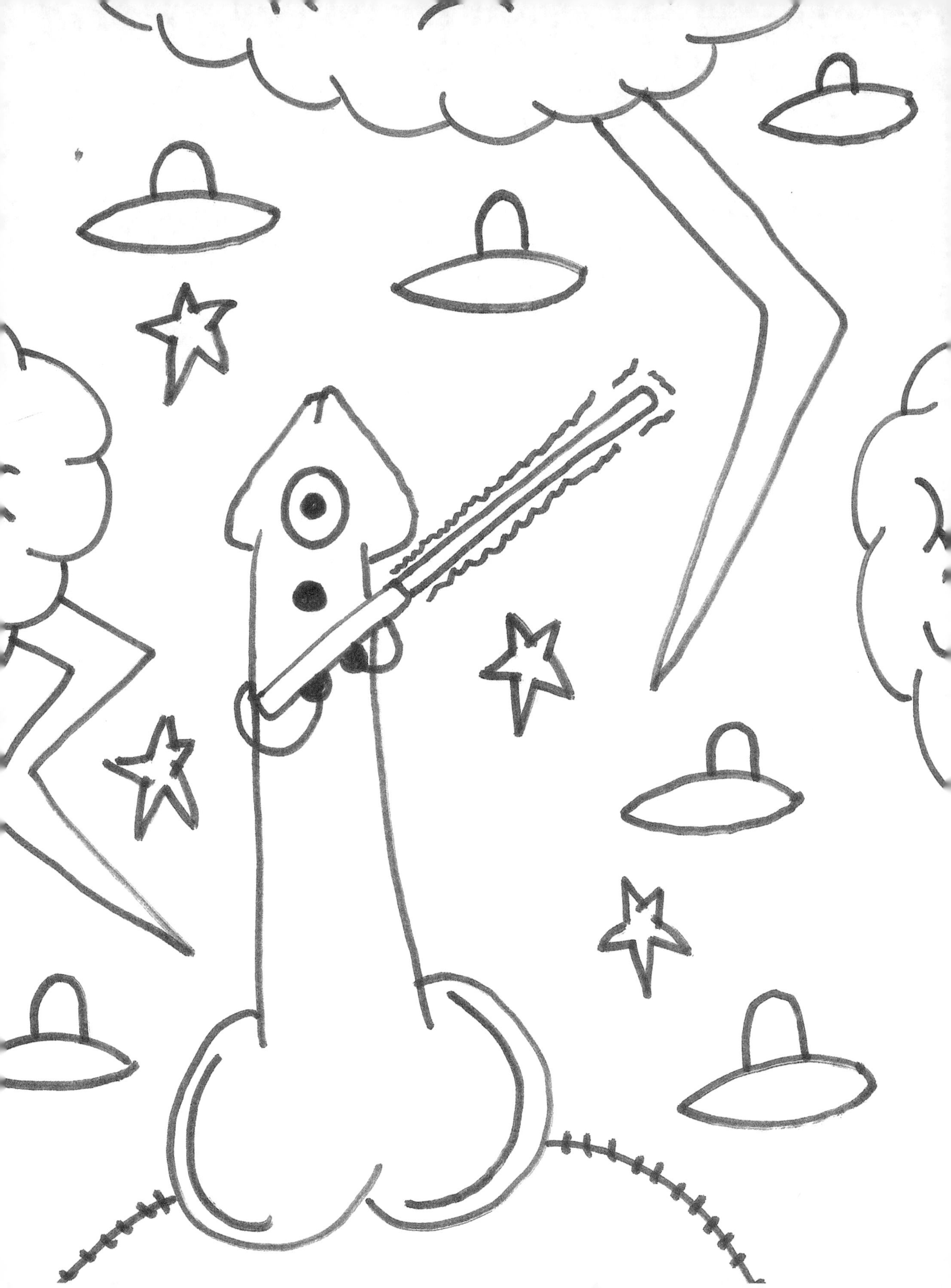

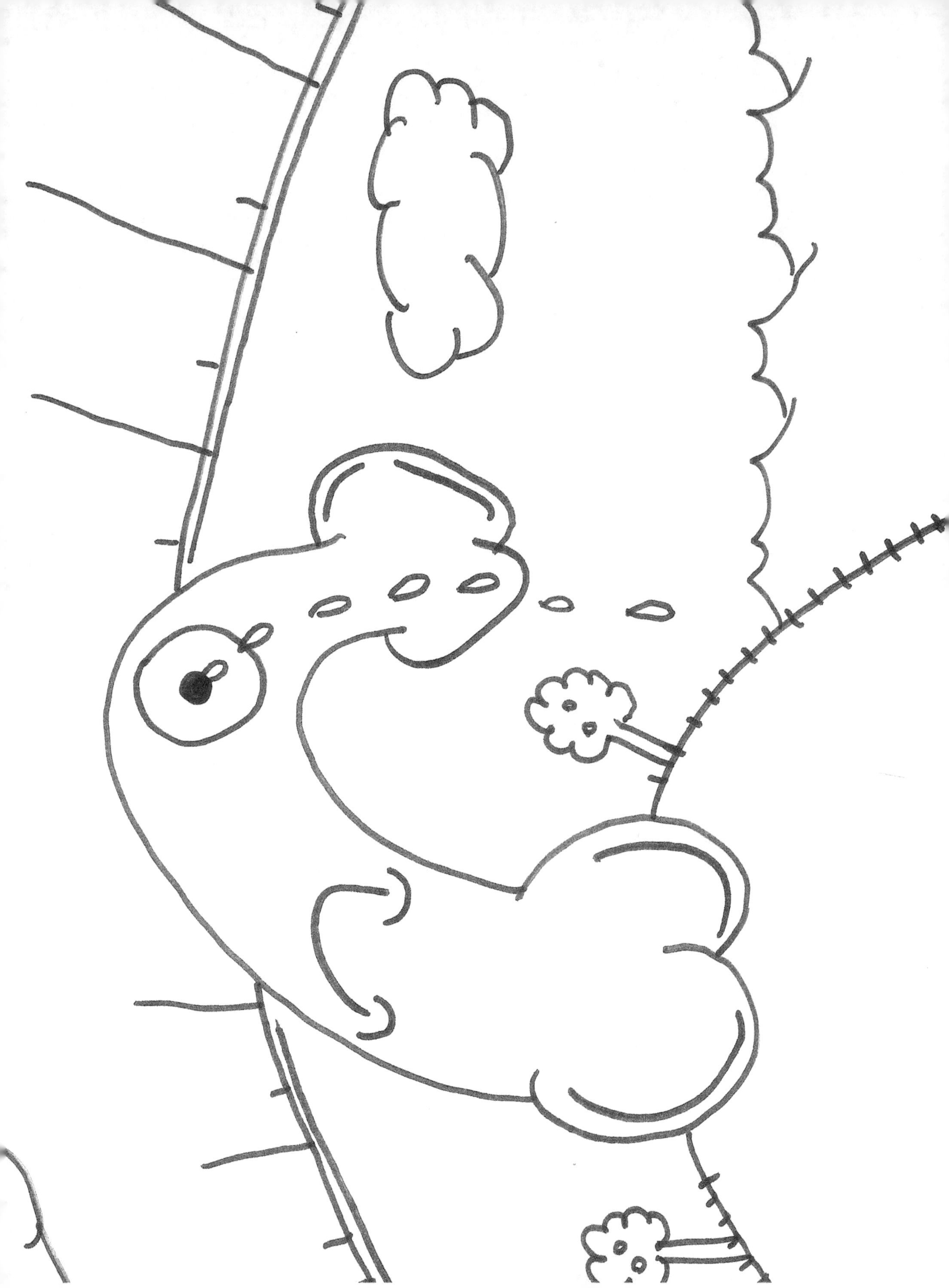

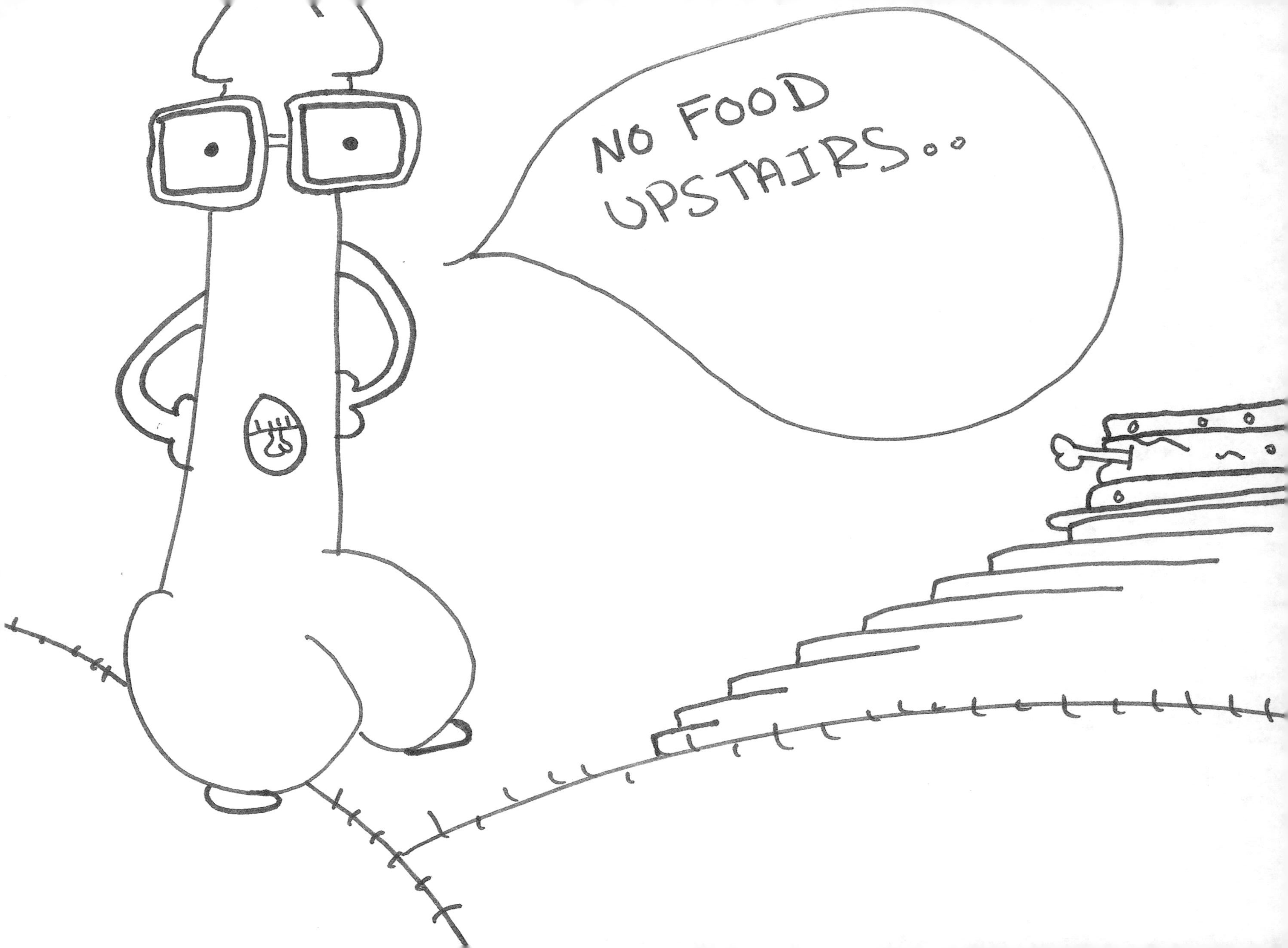
NO FOOD UPSTAIRS..

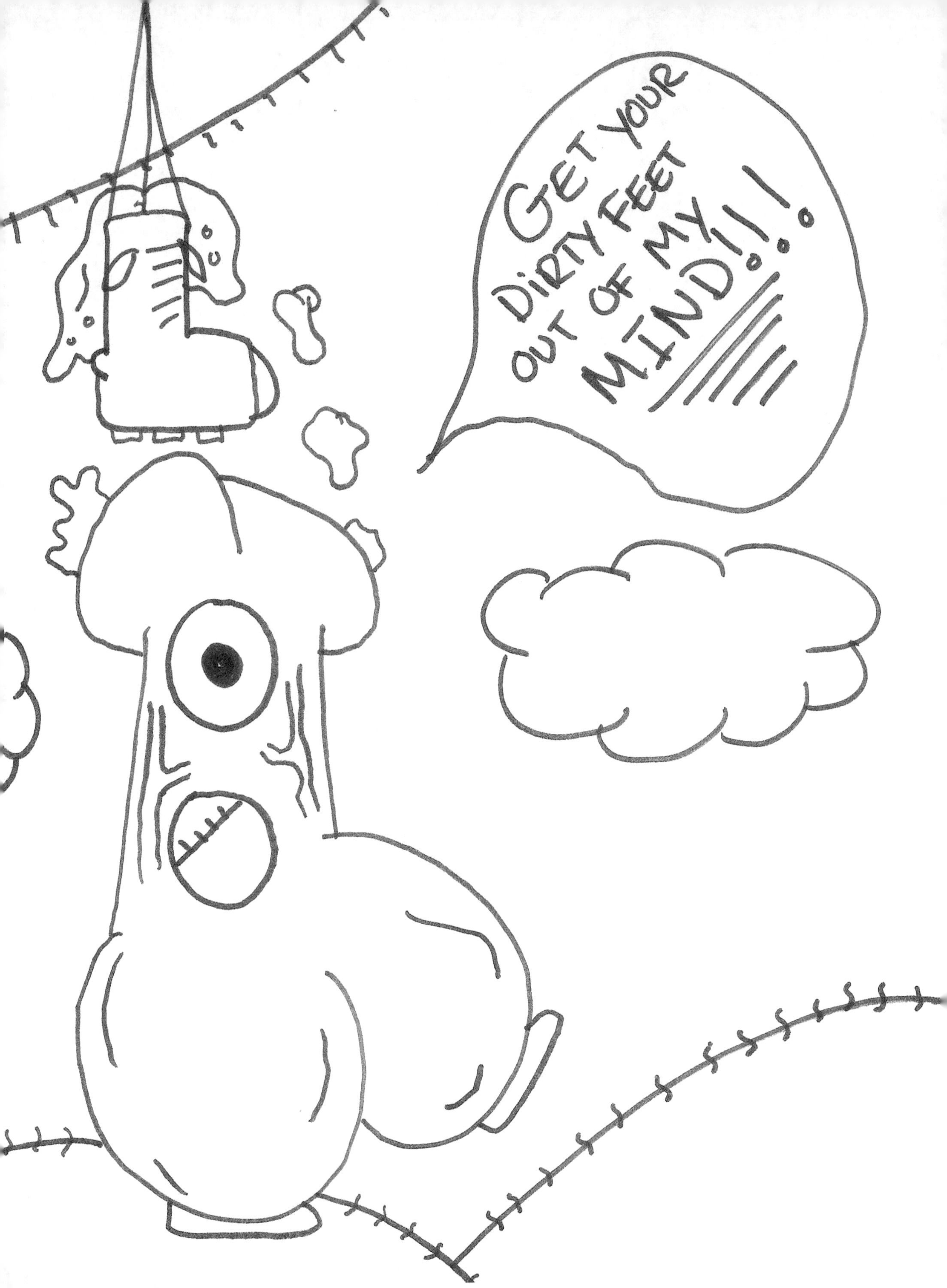
GET YOUR DIRTY FEET OUT OF MY MIND!!!

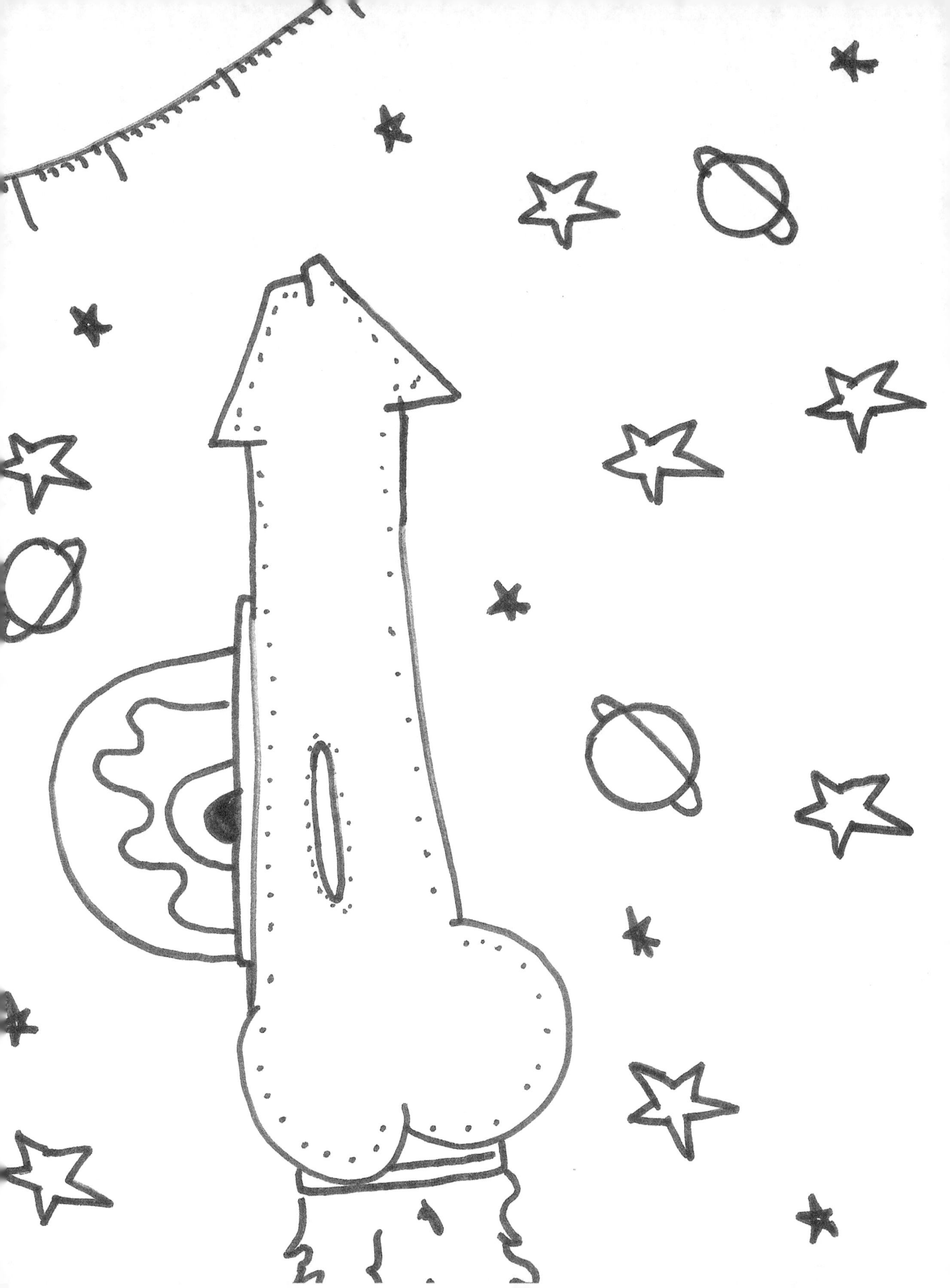

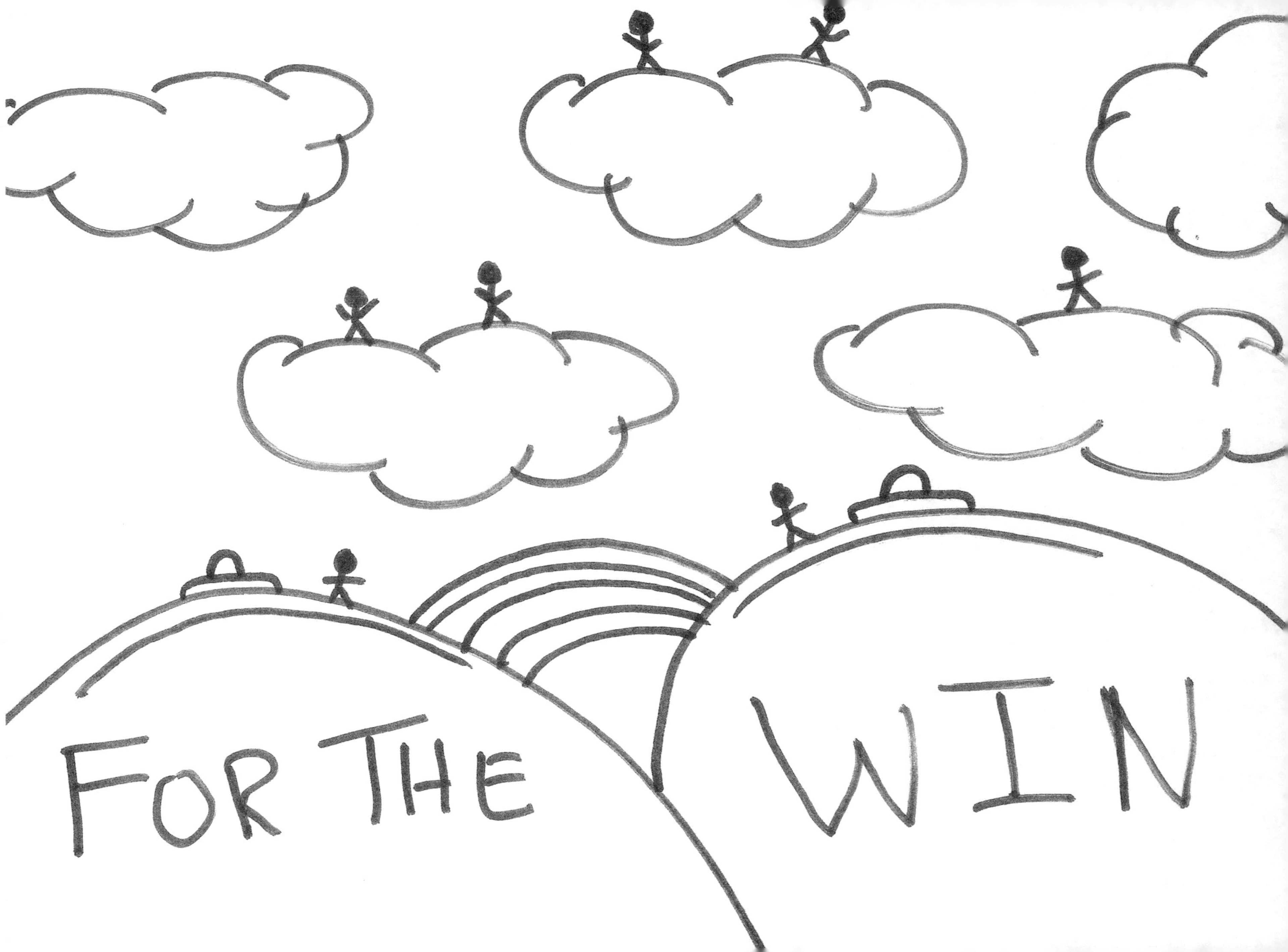
FOR THE WIN

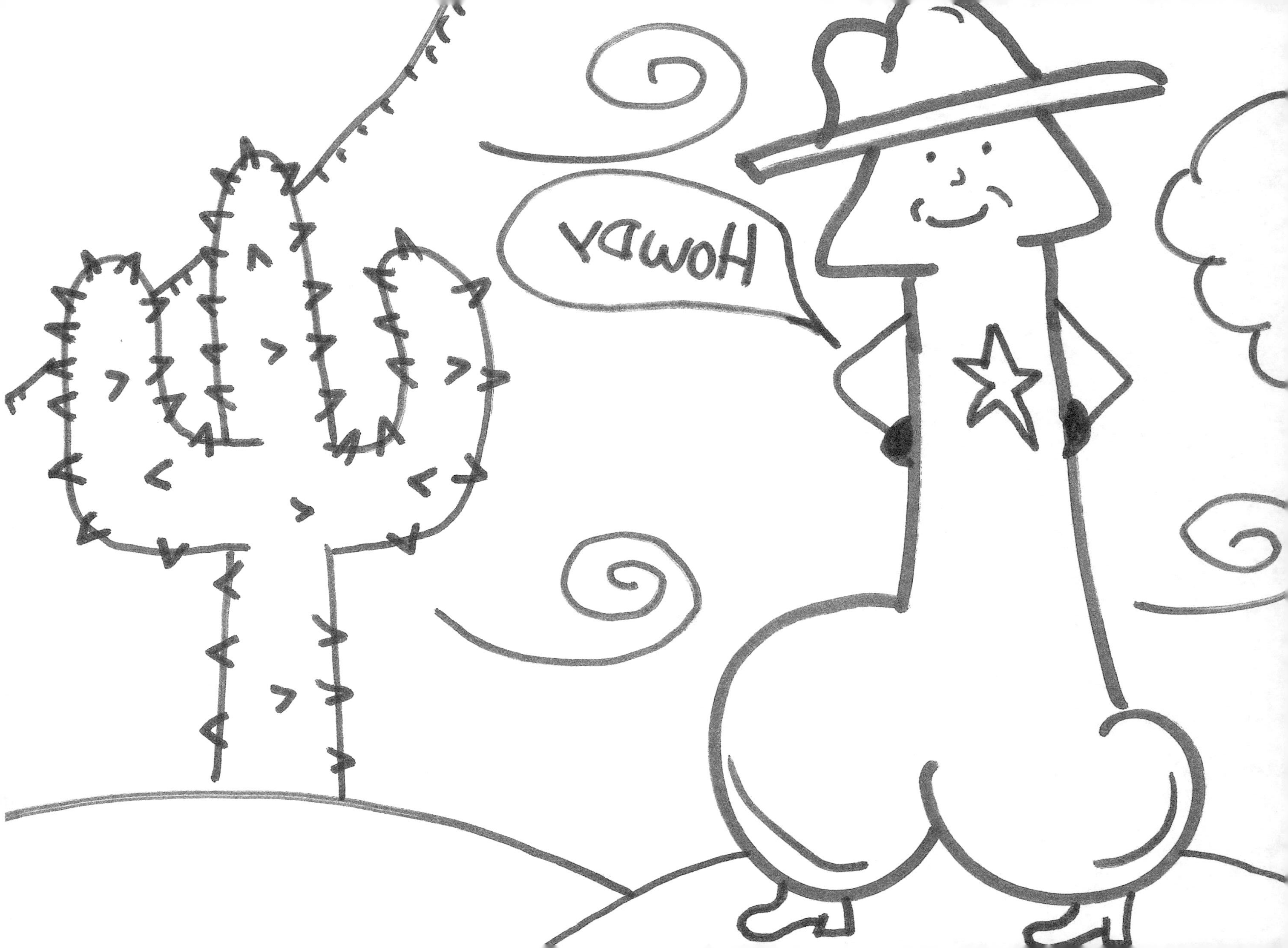
HOWDY

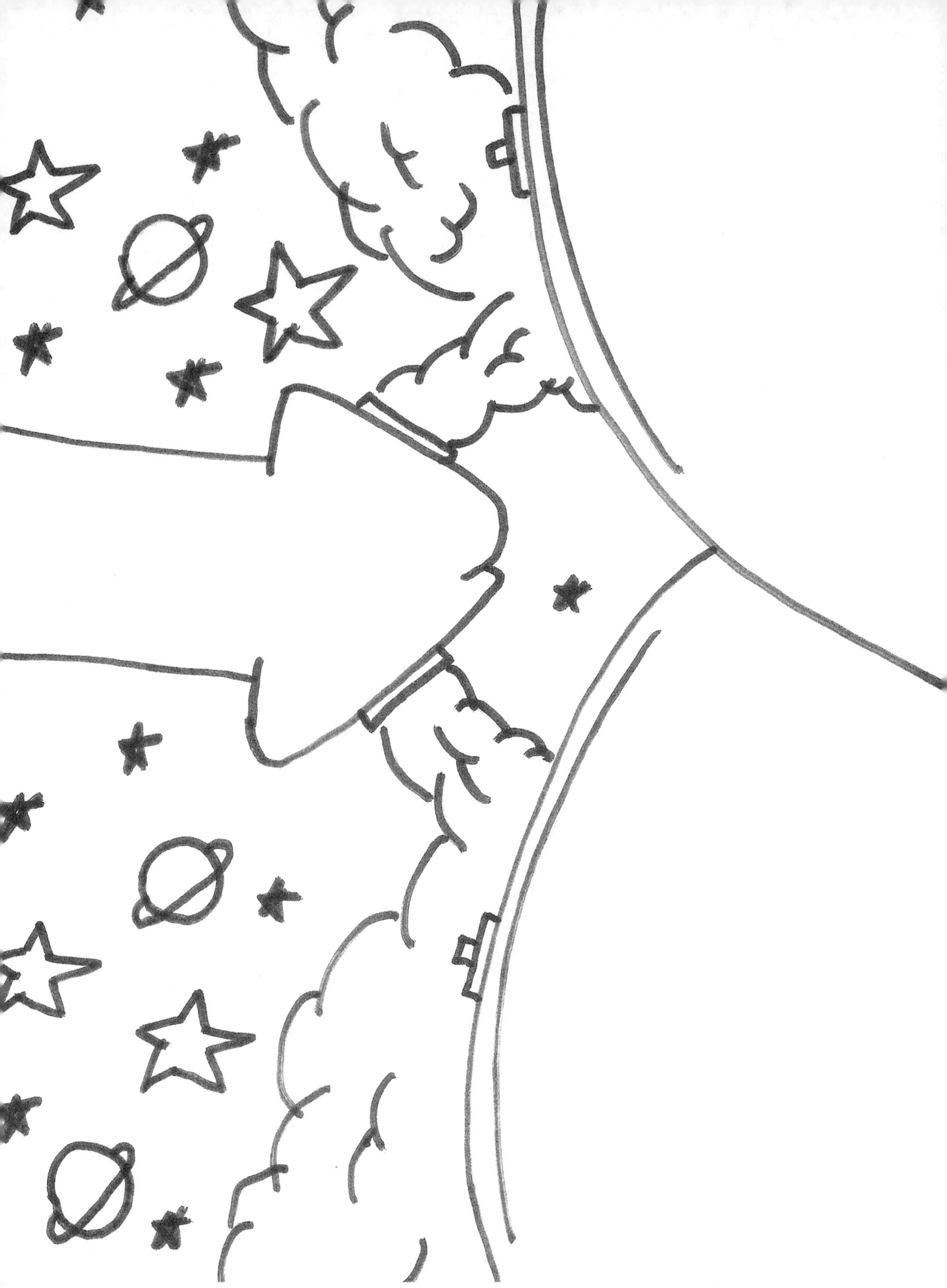

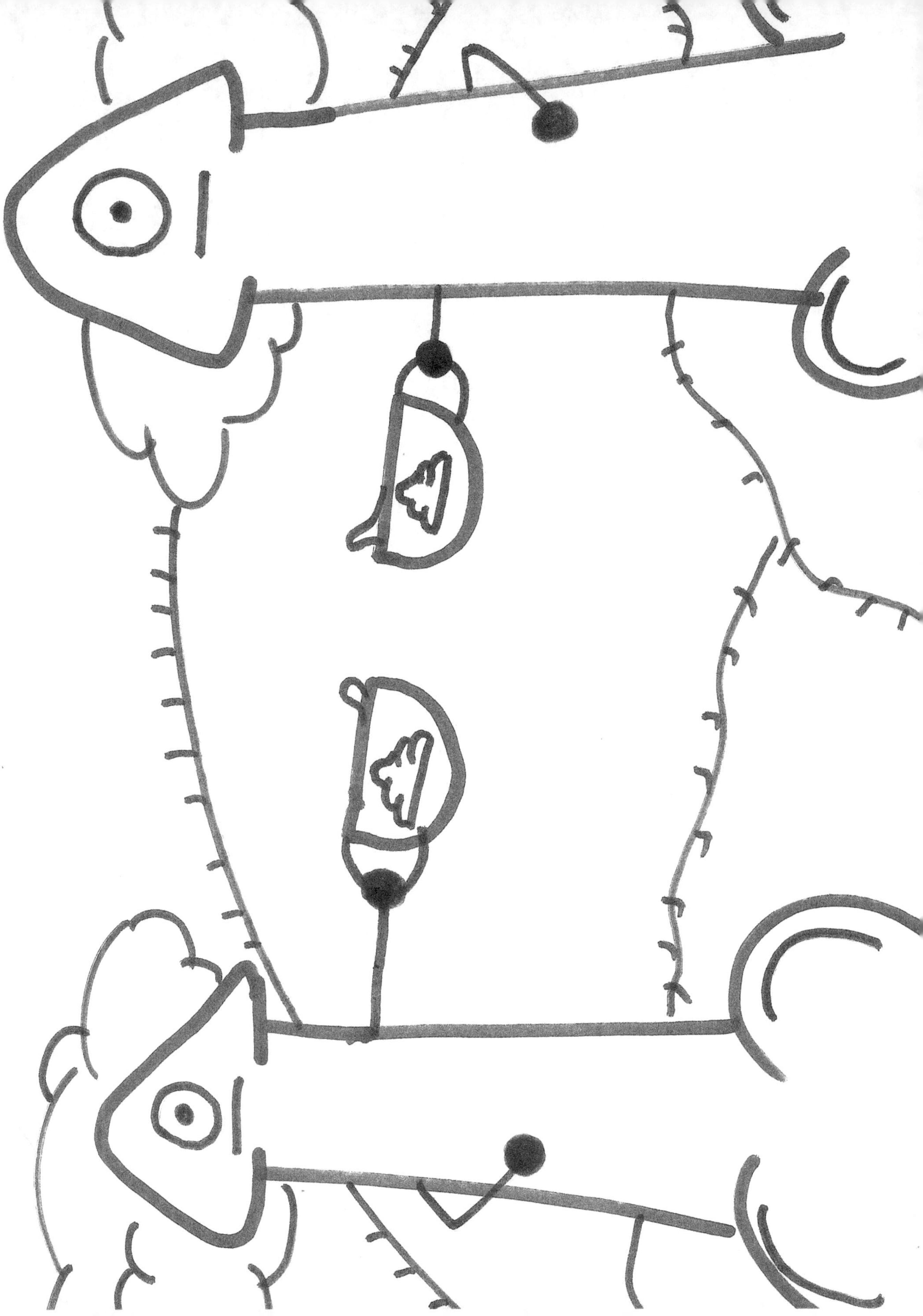

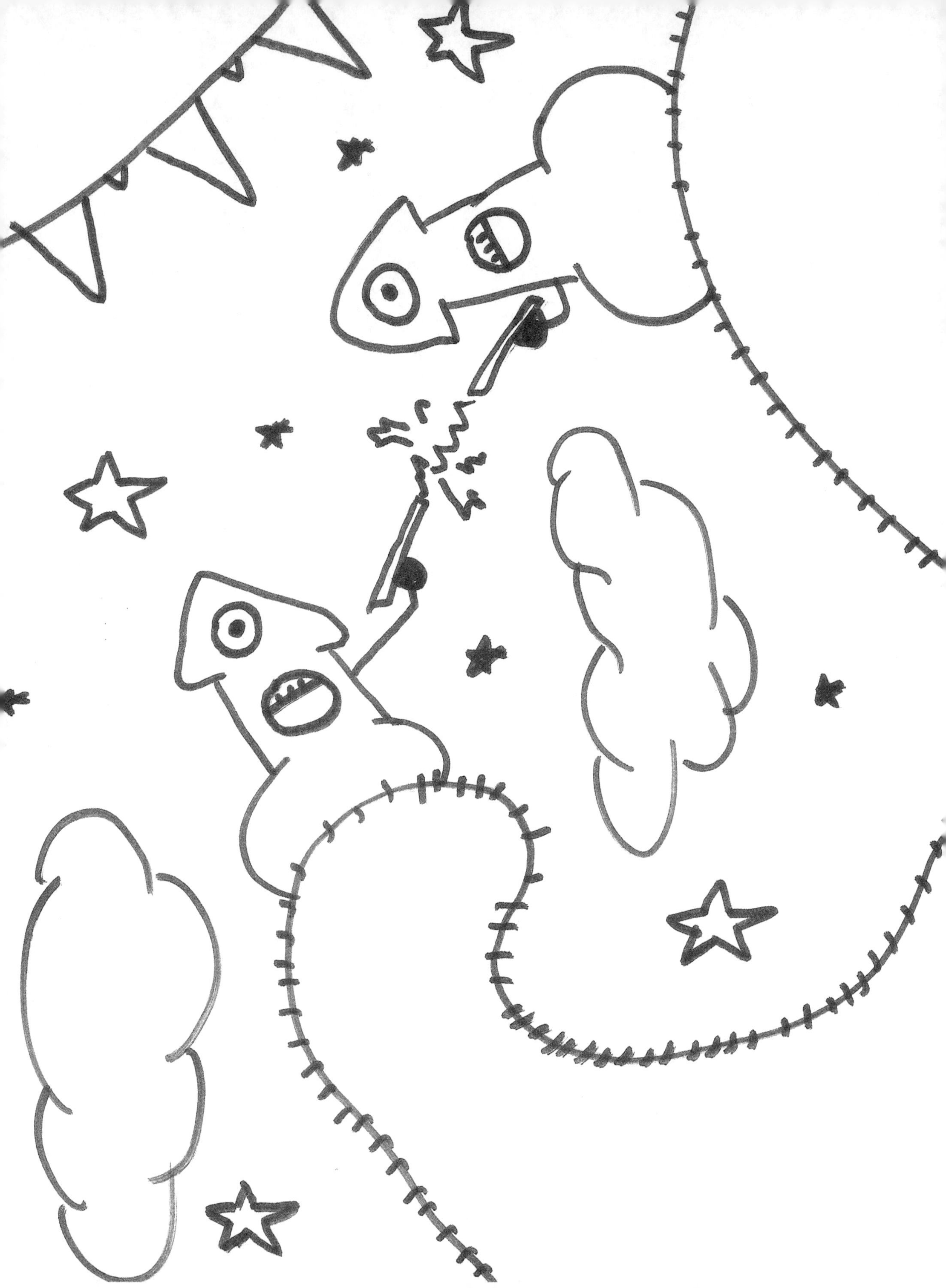

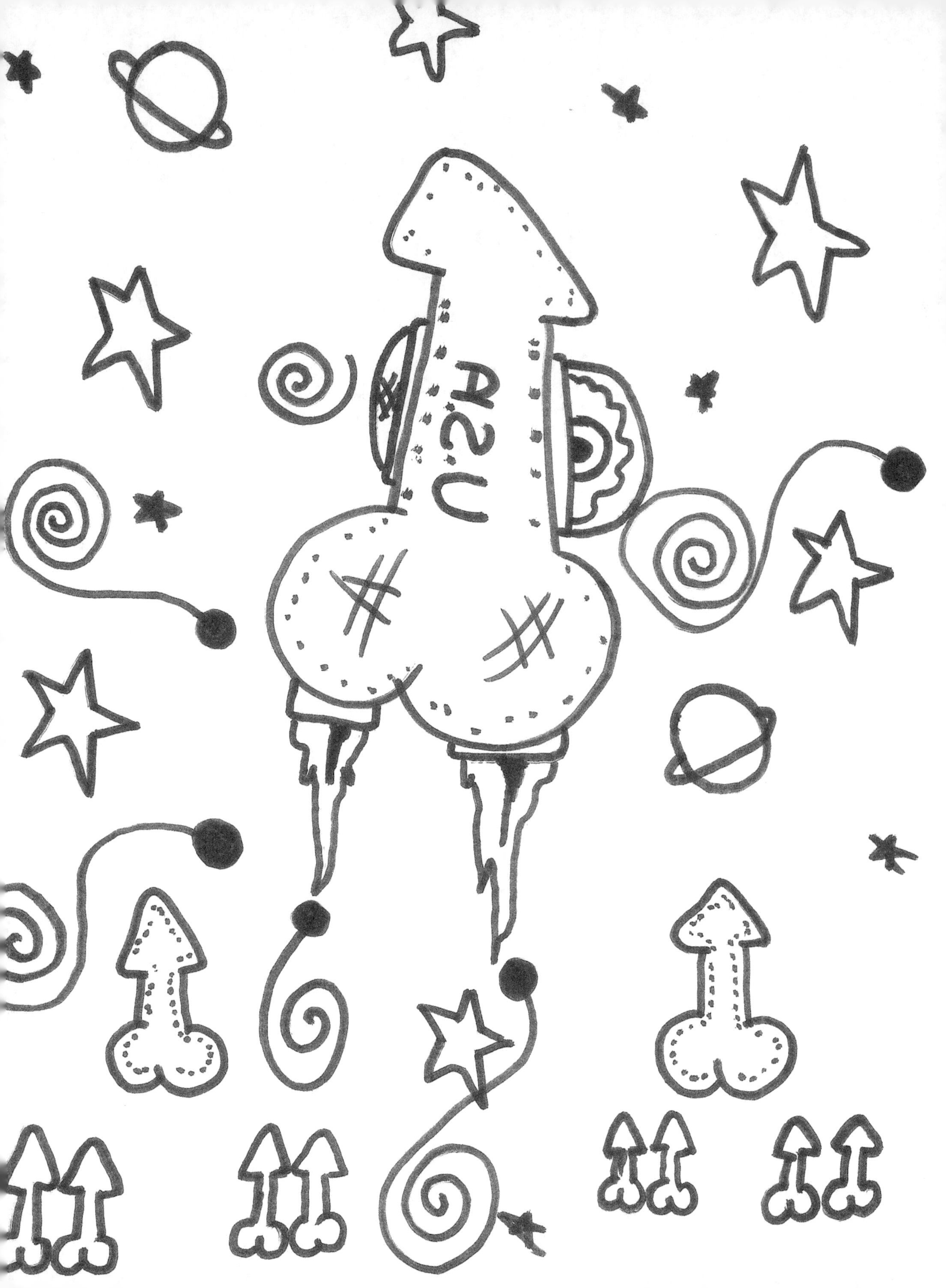

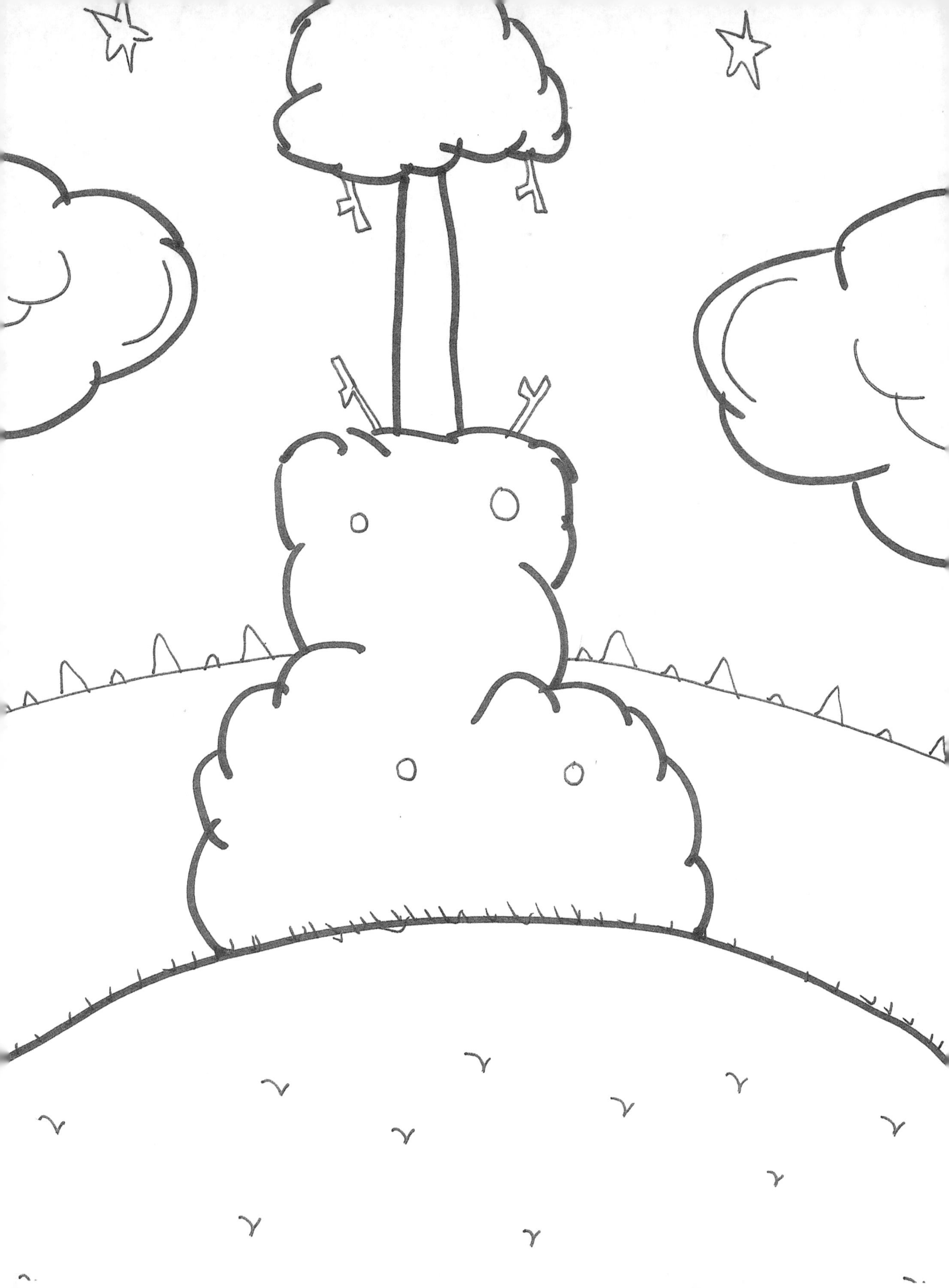

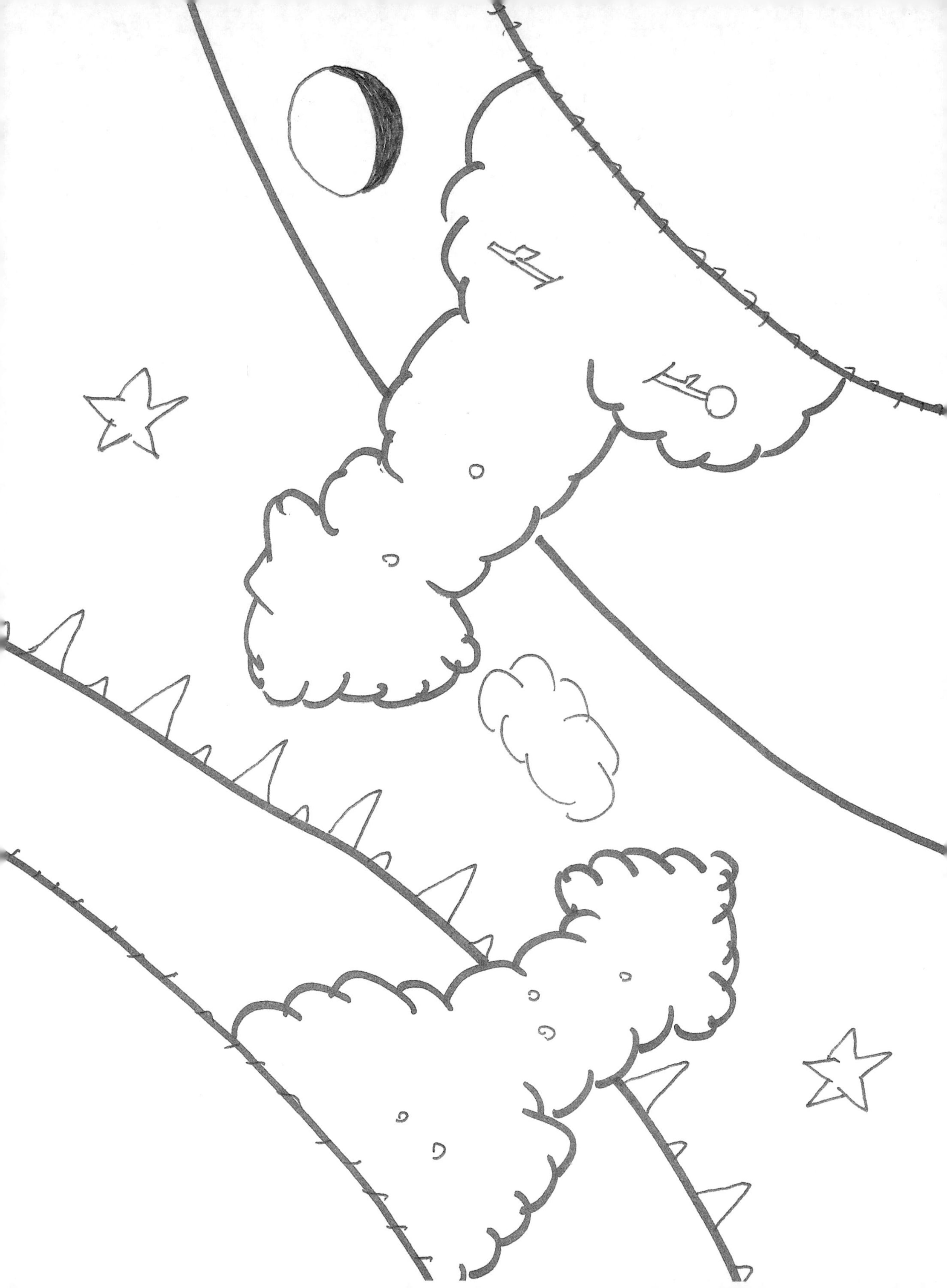

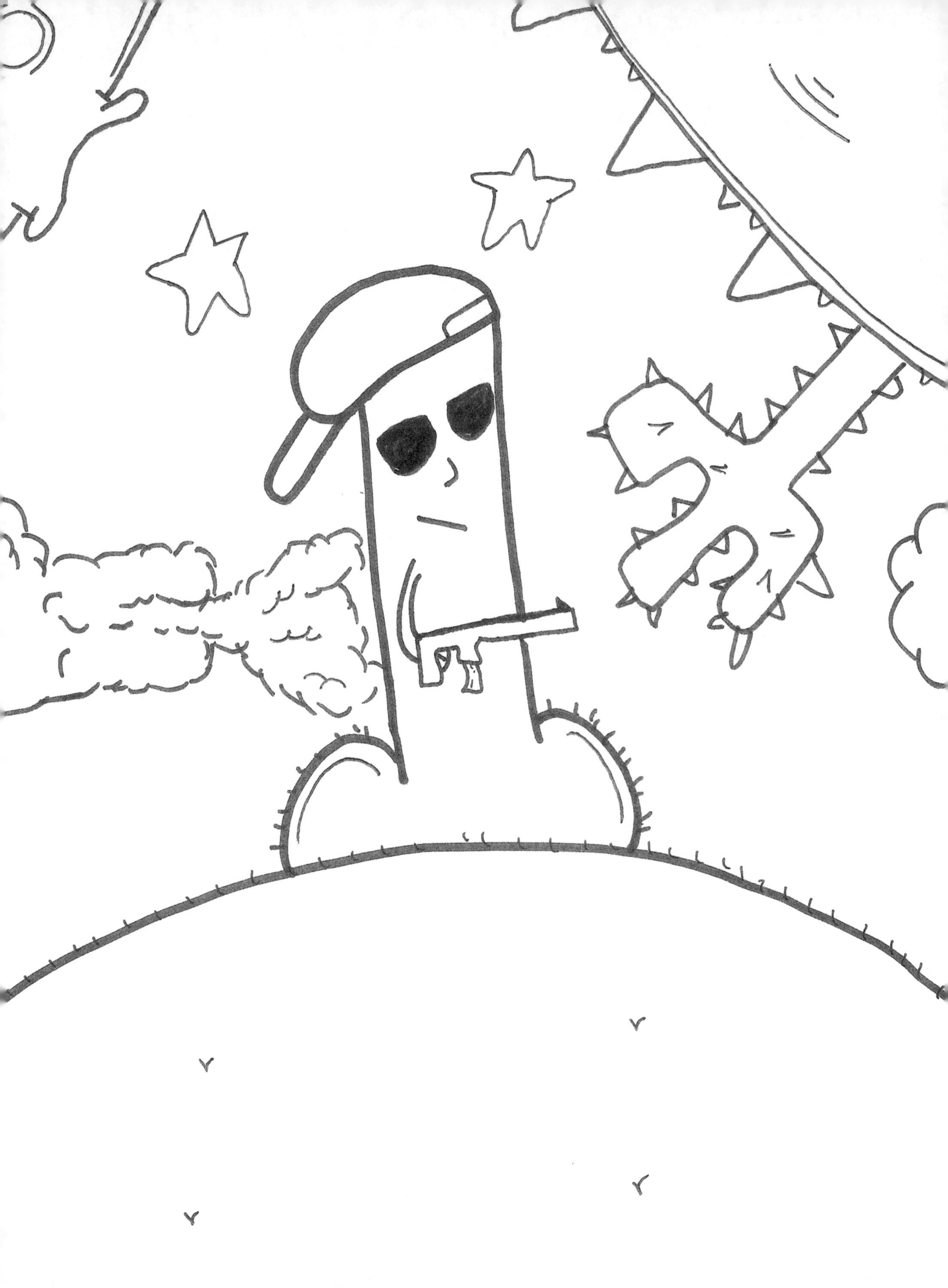

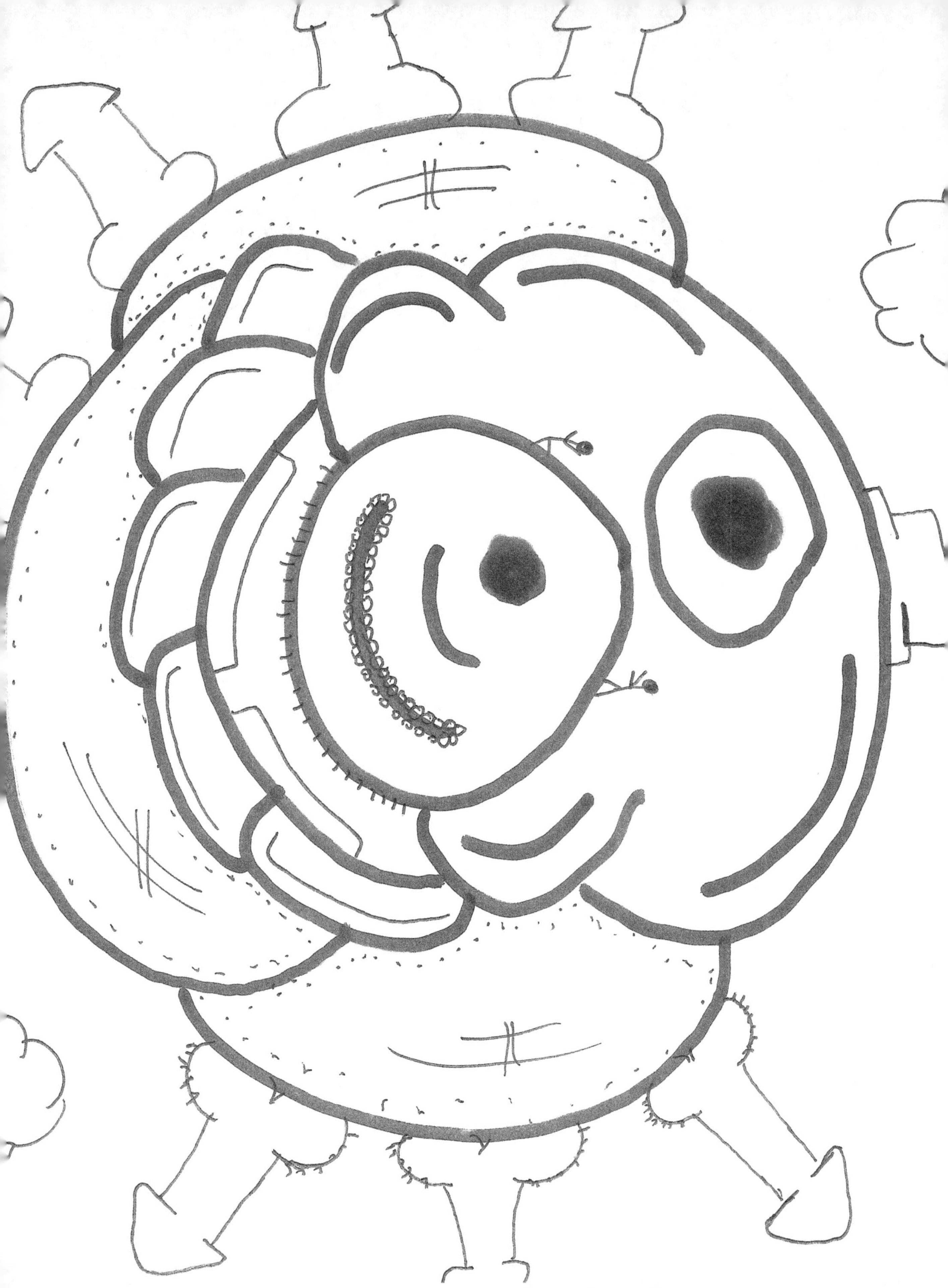

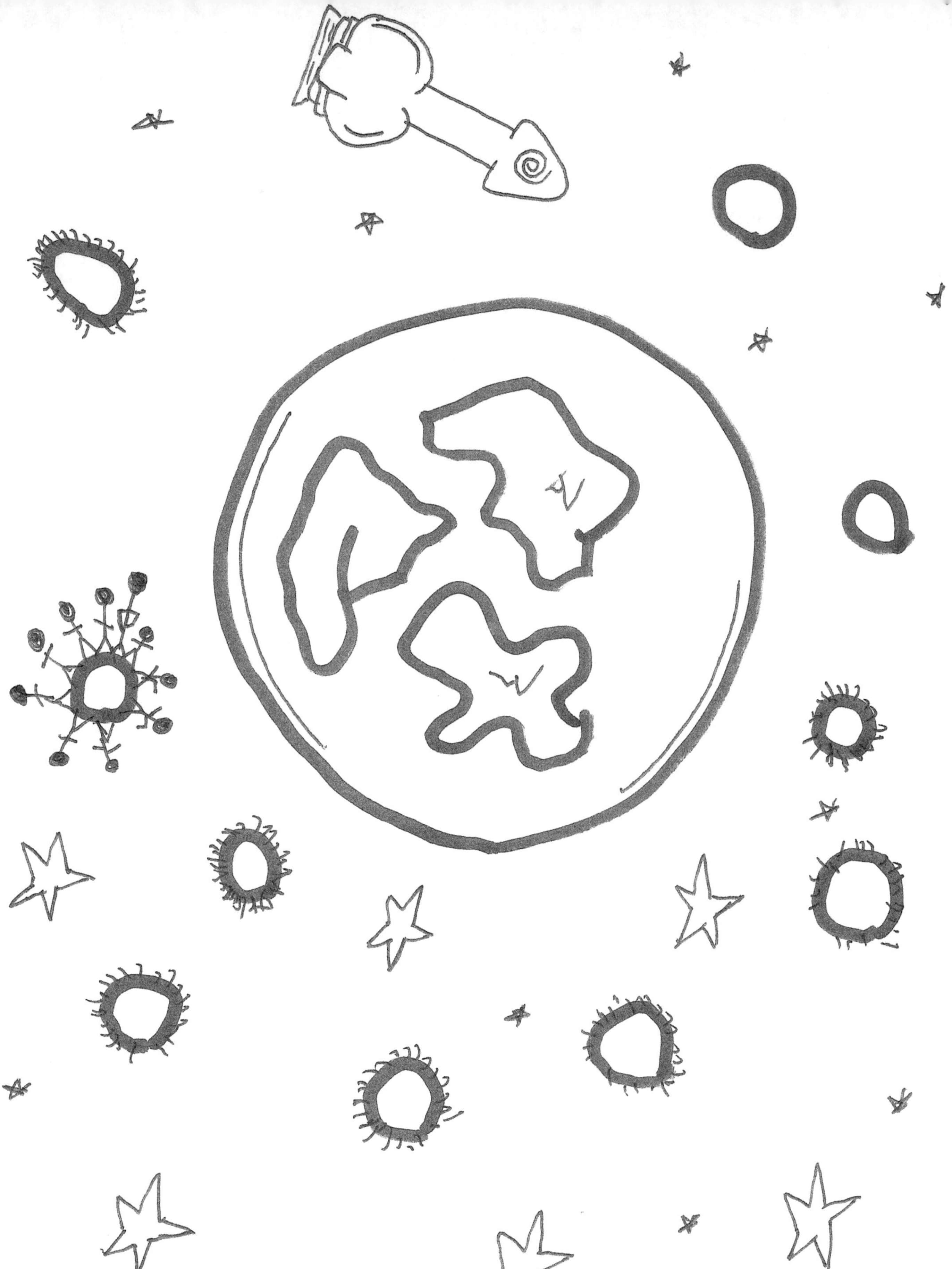

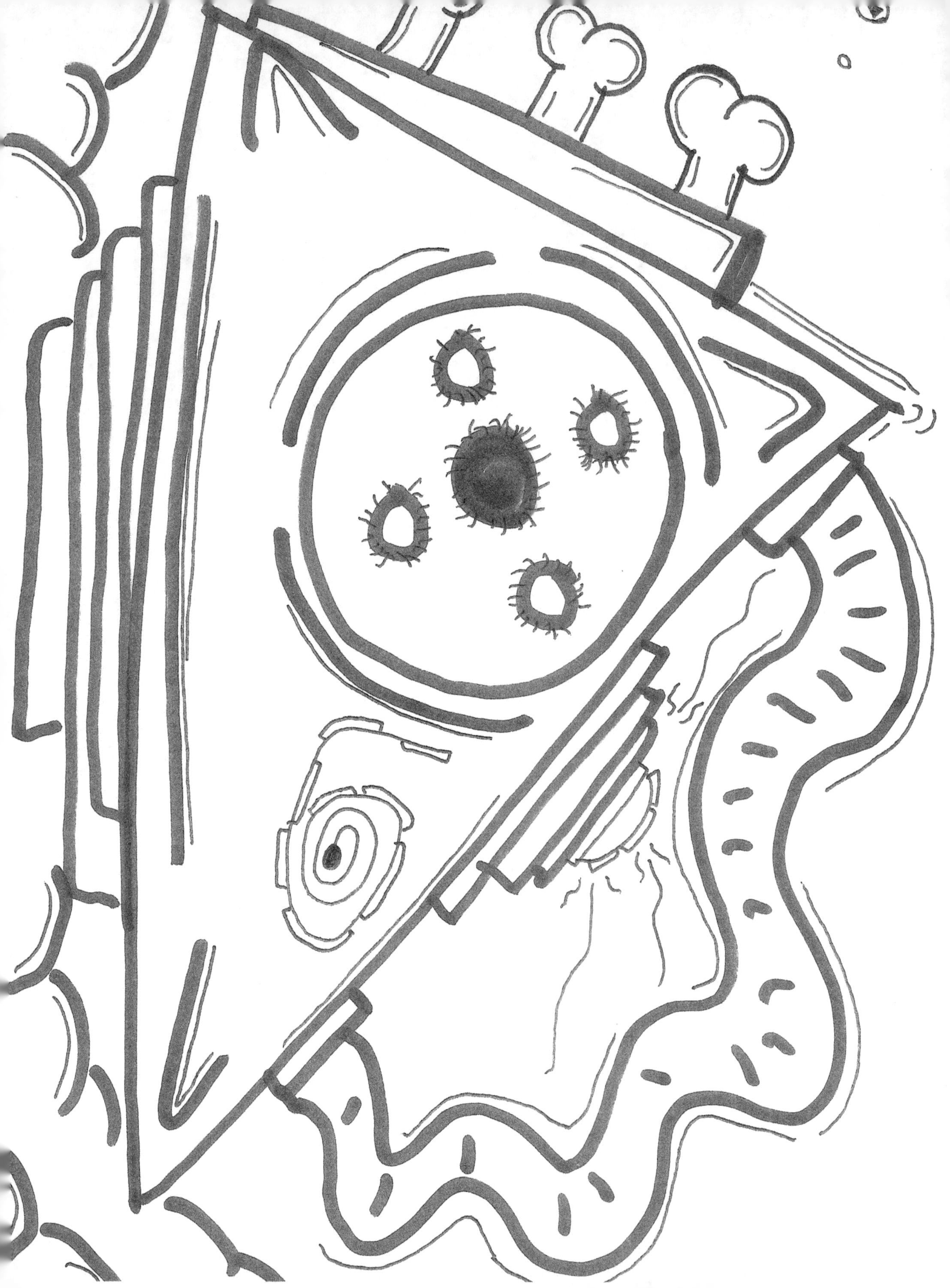

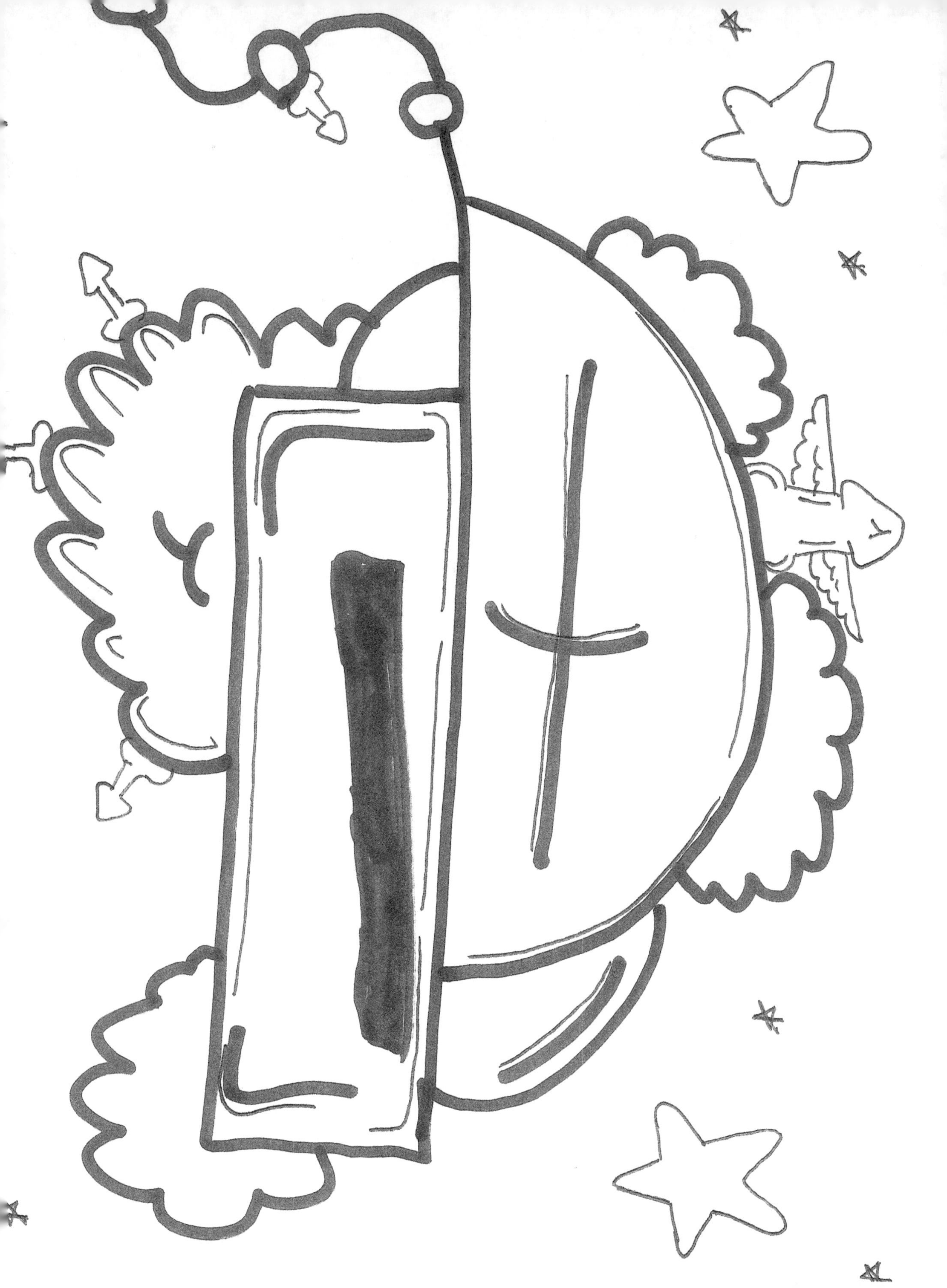

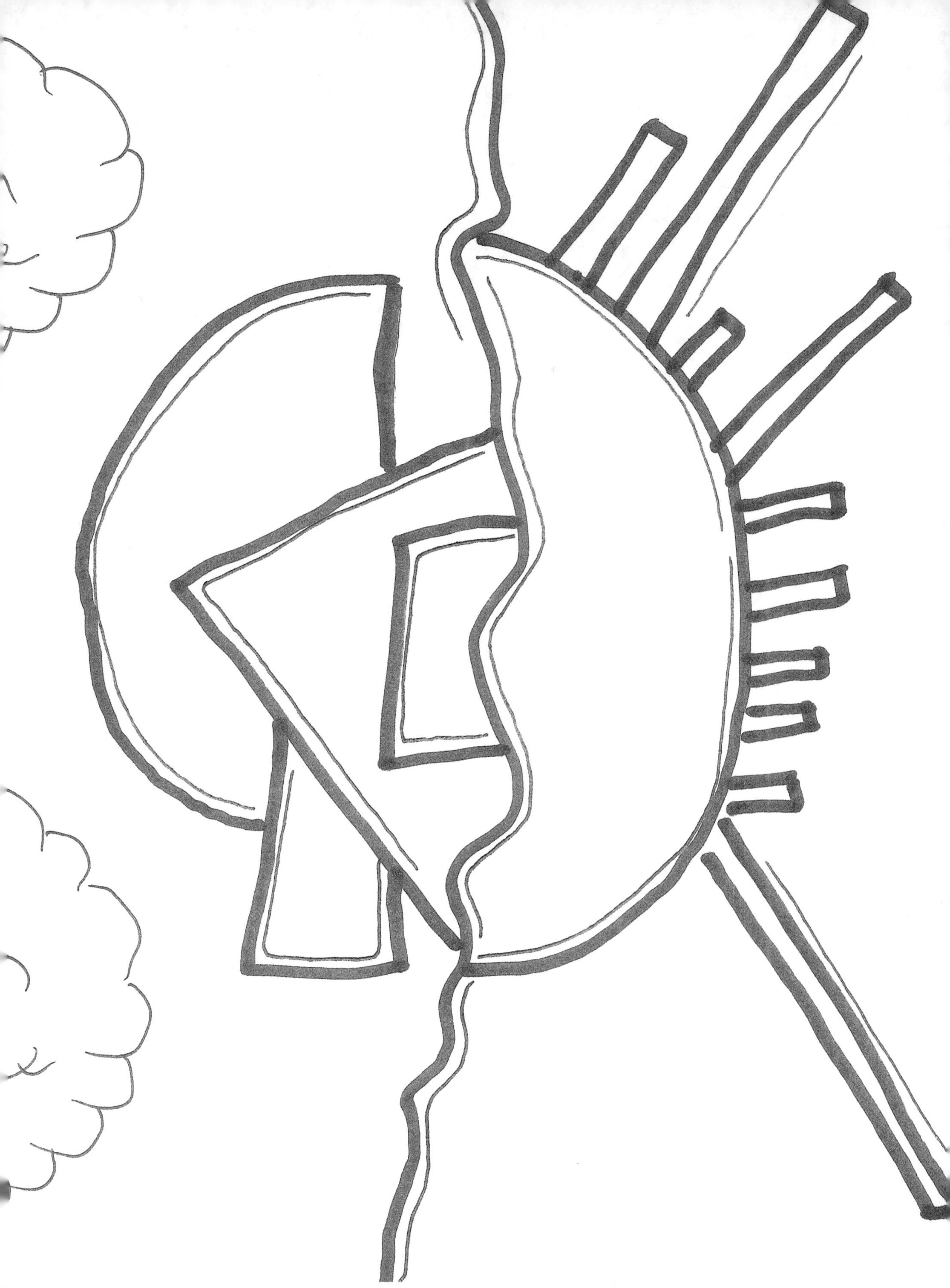

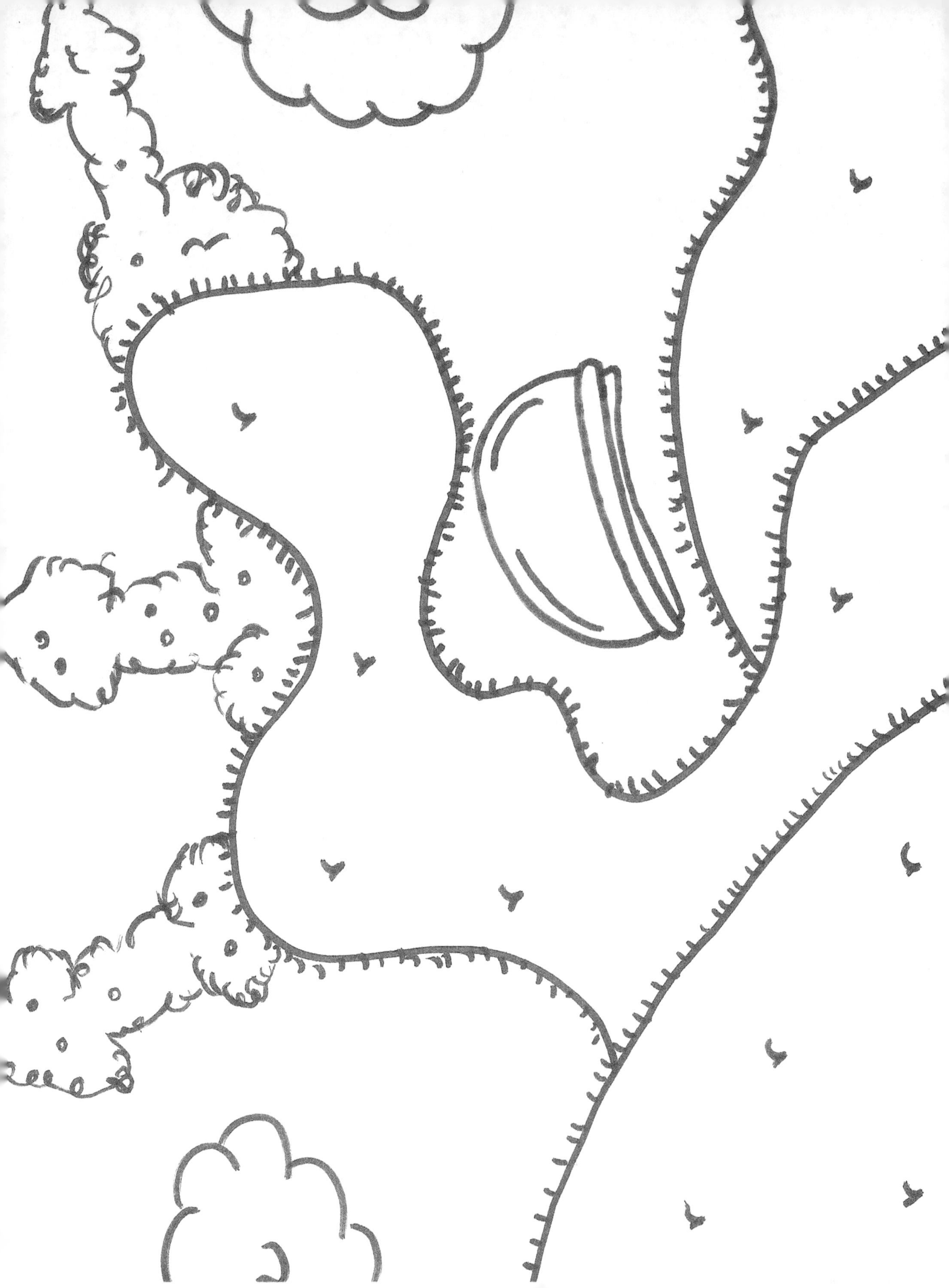

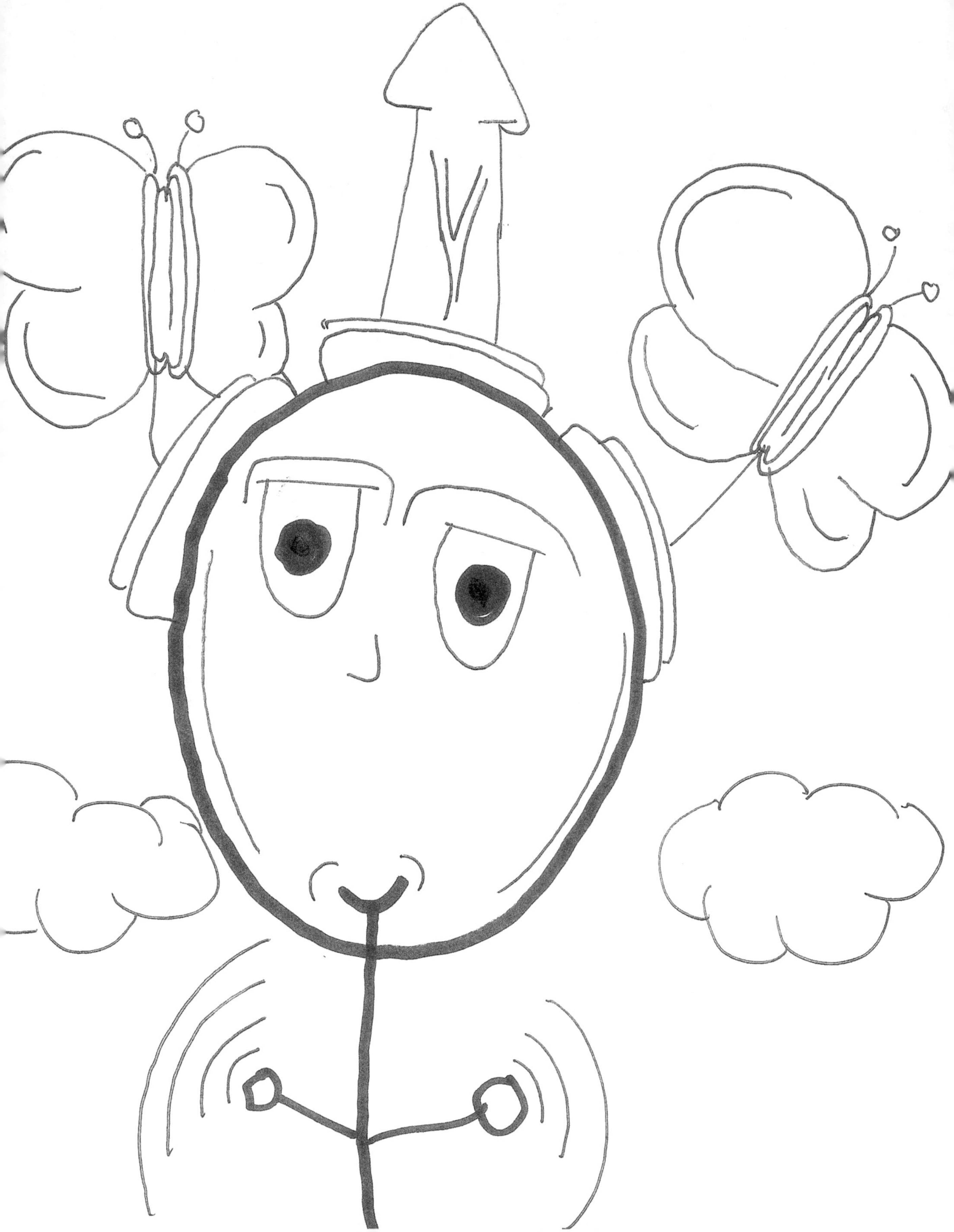

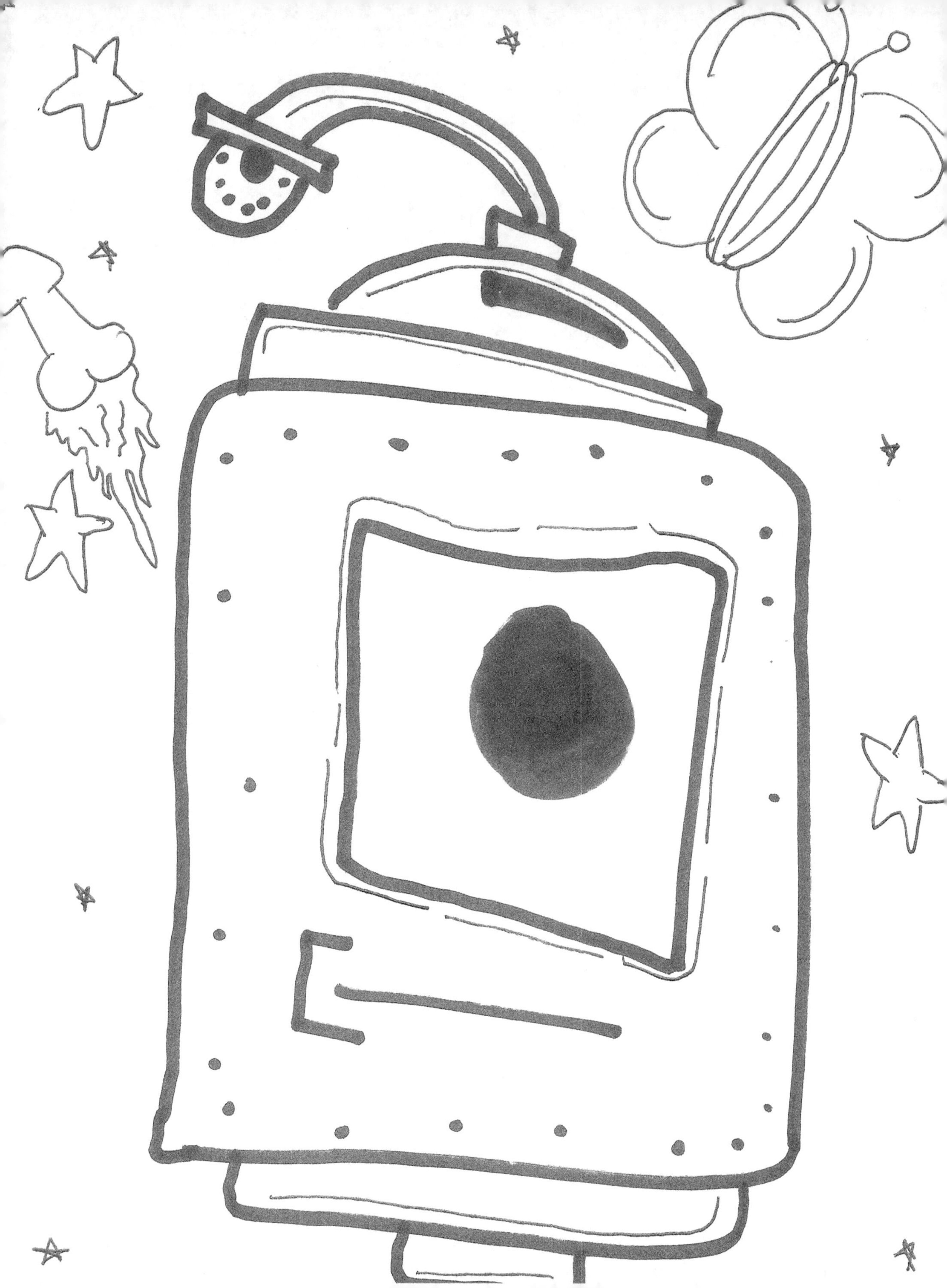

www.ingramcontent.com/pod-product-compliance
Lightning Source LLC
Chambersburg PA
CBHW080308180526
45167CB00006B/2723
* 9 7 8 1 4 9 4 4 1 8 6 1 8 *